Sweet Debbie's

ORGANIC TREATS

ALLERGY-FREE & VEGAN RECIPES

from the

FAMOUS LOS ANGELES BAKERY

Sweet Debbie's
ORGANIC TREATS
ALLERGY-FREE & VEGAN RECIPES
from the
FAMOUS LOS ANGELES BAKERY

Debbie Adler
Owner, Sweet Debbie's Organic Cupcakes

PHOTOGRAPHY BY CARL KRAVATS

HARLEQUIN
www.Harlequin.com

www.Harlequin.com

Sweet Debbie's Organic Treats

ISBN-13: 978-0-373-89282-2

© 2013 by Debbie Adler

The health advice presented in this book is intended only as an informative resource guide to help you make informed decisions; it is not meant to replace the advice of a physician or to serve as a guide to self-treatment. Always seek competent medical help for any health condition or if there is any question about the appropriateness of a procedure or health recommendation.

All photography by Carl Kravats except cover photograph and photograph on page x. Photograph on page x by Michael Paul/Getty Images.

CIP Data available upon request.

www.Harlequin.com

Printed in U.S.A.

Little did I expect that
my life's purpose would come
in the form of a blue-eyed,
button-nosed bundle of boy.
This book is dedicated to him.

CONTENTS

INTRODUCTION

I wasn't always into health food. Back in my corporate days I would often eat frozen yogurt for lunch and cookie dough ice cream as an after-dinner chaser and think nothing of it. That is, until I started to look like Miss Piggy with an attaché case. Then it dawned on me that maybe I needed to rethink my choices.

I started to read all about the ill effects of refined white sugar on the body and realized my long-term prognosis wasn't good. So I set out to my local health food store to see if I could find some desserts made with alternative sweeteners. No go. I could not find one crumb of a cookie that did not contain evaporated cane juice (a fancy term for sugar).

I never thought of myself as a pioneer in anything, let alone baking, but I found myself in my kitchen that night with a boatload of all-natural, low-glycemic sweeteners and went to work. Mind you, I didn't know what I was doing, so it took a while to get anything edible to come out of the oven, but I was determined.

It took about a year, but after extensive research about nutrition and the science of baking, coupled with disastrous errors for which I should have been put on trial, I came up with an assortment of goodies containing only organic and healthful ingredients sweetened with stevia and coconut nectar.

And like most everything I do in my life, if it's tasty and smile-inducing, I have to share. So, in 2006 I opened my bakery, Sweet Debbie's Organic Cupcakes. And from day one, my Irresistible Red Velvet Cupcakes, imbued with fresh cranberries and lemon; my Oatmeal Fudge Chocolate Chip Cookies, filled with homemade dark chocolate chips; and my Cran Ban Thank You Bran Muffins, made with potassium-rich bananas and dried cranberries; among other Sweet Debbie's originals, started flying out the bakery door due to customer demand.

And just as I was enjoying the momentum, I found out—after several anaphylactic episodes—that my son has life-threatening allergies to almost every food in the USDA pyramid, except salt.

So in 2009 I went back into my kitchen, did some more research and experiments, and came up with gluten-free and allergy-free formulas for all the Sweet Debbie's menu items.

In that same year I revamped my bakery so it could be a safe haven for those with dietary restrictions similar to my son's, and against all odds, business increased exponentially. It is now the go-to bakeshop for anyone with an allergy or intolerance to dairy, eggs, soy, wheat, gluten, nuts and sugar, and for folks who are just plain hungry for a wholesome treat.

But soon I realized that there must be people out there who don't have access to my bakery and who might want to partake. And even though Sweet Debbie's ships its treats nationwide, I thought there might be some type A, paranoid individuals who don't trust *anyone* to make their snacks for them. Thus, I decided to write it all down.

So here you are (okay, maybe you're not necessarily paranoid and type A, or maybe you are, but it's nothing to be ashamed of). Here are my blow-by-blow lists of Must-Haves and Must Do's, my How-To's and What For's, so you will be well equipped to tackle any recipe in this book like a defensive linebacker donning an adorable apron.

By using the "clean" ingredients suggested in this book, you won't have to worry about having sugar rushes and crashes, or ingesting artificial colors, pesticides or preservatives. It means

you will never have to worry again about your food-allergic child being denied a cupcake or not having a fuel-filled energy bar to eat right before soccer practice. Above all, it means you can feel confident that the kick-it-up-a-notch, nutritious, allergen-free treats coming out of your oven will keep you and the members of your family healthy, happy and unharmed.

In the pages that follow, I explain why I use nourishing grapeseed oil and coconut oil; how and why it's best to sweeten with zero-calorie, all-natural stevia and mineral-rich coconut nectar; and how my gluten-free flour mix packs an alimental punch, and I offer a treasure trove of valuable tips, tricks and intimate details.

Many of the munchies in these pages are geared to kids in terms of taste, portion sizes, ease of handling and lunch-box compatibility, but there are a few treats in each chapter that are designed for you, my awesome reader, for whom I've developed some more sophisticated and grown-up indulgences.

And it is you, my fellow baker, with whom I share this gastronomical journey one hearty and satisfying nosh at a time. Let's dig in!

Debbie

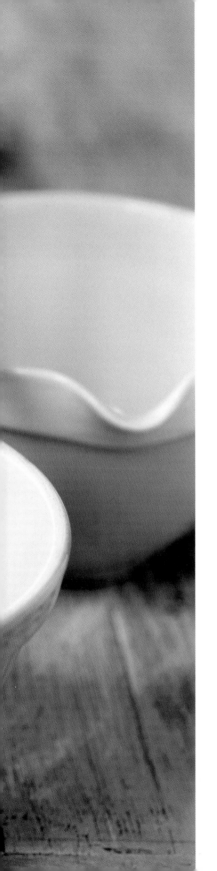

CHAPTER 1

FREE FOOD
FULLY LOADED

I've always loved grocery shopping. It makes me happy to be around so much food.

And now, more than ever before, I see all the "alternative" choices I used to be able to get only at health food stores hanging out on supermarket shelves, rubbing elbows with more mainstream fare.

Most of the ingredients you'll need to make these recipes are quite easy on the pocketbook. However, there are a few superfood prima donnas among them that boast a designer sticker price. I ask you to just think of them as your health insurance co-pay, because I promise you, none of them are pricier than the cost of getting sick.

Here you'll find a comprehensive list of almost everything you'll need to get started. After much analysis and testing, I chose each component based on its high nutritional value as well as baking functionality. So it is with great pleasure that I now introduce you to the cast.

Sorghum flour – contains a vast array of vitamins and minerals, including B_6, potassium, iron, magnesium, some vitamin E and antioxidants. Poor little sorghum used to compete with wheat flour for attention, but now he is more popular than ever because he's whole grain and gluten free.

Millet flour – is highly nutritious and includes the B-complex vitamins, iron, phosphorous and potassium. Since Miss Millet is very shy, it is not all that well known that she is considered the least allergenic and most digestible of all the gluten-free grains.

Quinoa flour – is queen in the gluten-free fiefdom because quinoa is a protein unto herself and thus doesn't need some gassy bean dude to complete her. She has the full amino acid collection and is spectacularly rich in potassium, iron, copper, manganese and calcium.

Teff flour – is a flour milled from teff, a teensy-weensy gluten-free grain that contains a powerhouse of nutrients, including calcium, thiamin and iron. Teff is very fashionable and comes in a variety of colors, ranging from dark brown to red to ivory. I use ivory due to its mild flavor and soft texture.

Tapioca flour – is derived from the cassava root and is high in calcium, phosphorous, potassium, magnesium and iron. A bit of a starchy fellow, tapioca is a good thickener.

Buckwheat flour – contains B vitamins, minerals, flavonoids and all eight essential amino acids. I like to buy buckwheat groats and then grind them in my coffee grinder. The resulting flour is lighter in color than store-bought buckwheat flour and tastes a little better in these recipes. I refer to this as "light buckwheat flour" in the recipes contained in this book.

Amaranth flour — has the good sense to contain not only the vitamins found in the previously mentioned gluten-free flours, but also elusive vitamin K, which is essential for good bone health. Amaranth is also high in lysine, a prominent amino acid in the amino acid community.

Rice bran — is a treasure chest of phytonutrients, fiber, iron, protein, vitamins B and E, and omega fatty acids. It is a key ingredient in my bestselling Cran Ban Thank You Bran Muffins.

Cornmeal — is considered a whole grain and contains a laundry list of nutrients, including niacin, thiamine, riboflavin, magnesium, phosphorus, potassium, zinc, and vitamins B_6, E and K. I use the coarse grind because of its exquisite texture and taste.

Cacao powder — contains important antioxidants, proteins and essential minerals. Some cacao powders are like a cheap date and may want to go Dutch, so stay away from them like the plague. Hook up with raw cacao powder, if possible.

Baking powder — is available gluten-free and sodium-free, and I'll tell you where you can get it in the resource section.

Guar gum — comes in handy quite often. Just when you think you're falling apart, Mr. Guar will save the day and hold it all together for you. He hails from a leguminous plant, so if that's an allergy issue, use xanthan gum instead.

Xanthan gum — is derived from a fermented polysaccharide. Xanthan is the better gum to use for yeasted goods and for pastries that contain a lot of citric acid.

Stevia powder — is a miraculous all-natural sweetener as it has zero calories and contains vitamins A and C, magnesium, zinc and iron.

Erythritol – sounds like an artificial chemical, but it is actually found in nature, in fruits and vegetables, and is an all-natural, zero-calorie sweetener. It does not promote tooth decay, is a free-radical-fighting antioxidant and is very easily digested. I use the powdered kind for the recipes in this book.

Coconut nectar – is a nutrient- and enzyme-dense, minimally processed, hypoallergenic, low-glycemic sweetener that contains seventeen amino acids, fiber, and vitamins B and C. How dare they call it a sap!

Chocolate chips – that is, the dark chocolate variety, are filled with antioxidants, vitamins and minerals. The higher the cacao content, the better. However, most packaged chocolate chips are only about 40 percent cocoa and are processed with refined sugar and soy lecithin. I will show you how easy it is to make dark chocolate chips with a high cacao content that are completely allergen free and sugar free.

Grapeseed oil – is an excellent source of antioxidants, plant sterols, vitamins C and E, as well as the essential fatty acids omega-3, omega-6 and omega-9.

Coconut oil – is considered one of the most desirable fats because it is nutrient dense and contains lauric acid, which has been shown to boost immunity. Coconut oil is a medium-chain fatty acid that gives the body an instant source of energy.

Vanilla extract – adds not only aromatics and flavor but also antioxidants to your baked goods. Just make sure you get the kind with no grain alcohol to guarantee it's gluten free.

Pumpkin seeds – are a good source of minerals, such as phosphorous, magnesium, manganese, copper, zinc and iron, as well as protein and vitamin K.

Sunflower seeds – contain a healthy dose of vitamins B_1, B_5 and E, as well as folate, copper, magnesium, selenium and phosphorous. Ms. Sunflower parades herself around as a seed but is technically a fruit.

Chia seeds – are nature's richest plant-based source of omega-3. They are supercharged with antioxidants, fiber, phytonutrients and proteins and are a great source of energy.

Hemp seeds – contain an alphabet soup of vitamins, all eight essential amino acids, and a perfect balance of the essential fatty acids omega-3 and omega-6, and they are a complete plant-based protein.

Rice milk – is always enriched with calcium and vitamin D and sometimes with vitamin B_{12}. I use the kind that is unsweetened and made with organic whole grain brown rice.

Coconut milk – is now available in many flavors and in shelf-stable cardboard containers of different sizes. It is enriched with calcium, folate, magnesium, selenium and vitamins B_{12} and D.

Coconut milk yogurt – is fortified with life-enhancing probiotics and is now abundantly available in a wide rainbow of flavors, but for the purposes of this book, I use the plain.

CHAPTER 2

HOW-TO'S & WHAT FOR'S

Please follow me as I show you the techniques I use to make my baked goods. Once you get the hang of it, you'll see how easy and fast it is to whip up a batch of my muffins, brownies, cookies, cupcakes, energy bars and donut holes. The breads take a little more patience because of the rising time, but don't be intimidated by the yeast. He is not a beast and is really very friendly. But if at first you don't succeed, bake and bake again. That's what I do to this day. Trust me, your efforts will be greatly rewarded.

Frosting Technique

Instead of using the traditional offset spatula to frost our cupcakes, donut holes and brownies, we use the precious espresso spoon. The little oval head is the perfect shape for swirling the frosting around and around and creating nice grooves.

Mixing Technique

It's important to keep in mind that with gluten-free flour, there's really no such thing as overmixing. So when incorporating ingredients, take the extra time to stir and stir again until you are sure that everyone is mingling and getting along in the batter.

Wrapping Technique

When wrapping the baked goods for freezer storage, make sure that the packages are really airtight to keep out any moisture.

Sweetening Technique

The sweeteners I use in my recipes require certain handling to do what they do best.

Stevia Powder

When stevia powder comes out of her bottle, she tends to get all over the place. So in order to avoid a white powder cloud in your face, add stevia to the recipe's liquid ingredients and stir well to combine, making sure the stevia is thoroughly incorporated.

Coconut Nectar

Since coconut nectar is thick and sticky, measuring it can be tricky. The spout can get a little bit messy, so I suggest you unscrew the bottle cap and the attached spout and then pour straight from the bottle. Always measure coconut nectar in an oiled measuring cup so that it will slip out easily and completely.

Recipes within My Recipes

If you'd like to bake as "cleanly" as possible, it helps to make your seed butters, chocolate chips and gluten-free flour mix from scratch. Here are the recipes for these.

HEMP SEED BUTTER

Makes almost 2 cups of seed butter

MUST HAVE

2 cups hemp seeds

4-5 tablespoons grapeseed oil

Sweet Truth:

If you don't want to heat your hemp seeds, you can make this seed butter without toasting. The resulting butter will be green, not brown.

MUST DO

1. Place the hemp seeds in a large frying pan over medium-low heat and toast them for about 4 minutes. Let them cool.

2. Grind the toasted hemp seeds in a coffee grinder or food processor until a powder forms.

3. Place the powder in a medium-size bowl, add the grapeseed oil a little at a time and stir until combined.

Store the hemp seed butter in an airtight container in the refrigerator so it stays fresh longer.

SUNFLOWER SEED BUTTER

Makes almost 2 cups of seed butter

MUST HAVE

15 x 10-inch sheet of parchment paper
2 cups raw sunflower seeds
4-5 tablespoons grapeseed oil

MUST DO

1. In order to get ground sunflower seeds to mimic peanut butter as closely as possible in color and flavor, roast the sunflower seeds in the oven before grinding.

2. Preheat oven to 275°F. Line a 15 x 10-inch jelly-roll pan with parchment paper.

3. Spread the sunflower seeds out in a single layer in the pan. Roast in the oven for 30–35 minutes, or until the sunflower seeds turn light brown, stirring halfway through roasting.

4. Take the pan out of the oven and let the seeds cool.

5. Grind the sunflower seeds in a coffee grinder or food processor until a powder forms. Place the powder in a medium-size bowl, add the grapeseed oil a little at a time and stir until combined.

Store the sunflower seed butter in an airtight container in the refrigerator so it stays fresh longer.

DARK CHOCOLATE CHIPS

Makes about 8 ounces of chocolate chips

MUST HAVE

15 x 13-inch sheet of parchment paper

4 ounces 100 percent cacao unsweetened chocolate bar

2 tablespoons coconut oil

6 tablespoons coconut nectar

¼ cup powdered erythritol

¼ teaspoon stevia powder

⅛ teaspoon fine sea salt

Sweet Truth:

To make the cutouts to top the cupcakes, as seen in some of the photos, pour the melted chocolate into chocolate candy trays in whatever shape you want to make. These trays can be bought in any candy supply or cake-decorating store. Place the trays in the freezer for about an hour, or until the chocolate hardens completely, and then just pop the shapes out.

MUST DO

1. Line a 15 x 13-inch cookie sheet with parchment paper.

2. Chop the chocolate into chunks, place them in a medium-size microwave-safe bowl with the coconut oil and microwave 30 seconds at a time until the chocolate melts.

3. Add the coconut nectar, powdered erythritol, stevia and salt and stir to combine. Set this aside to cool slightly.

4. Cut off a small tip of a disposable pastry bag or the corner of a gallon-size ziplock Baggie. Place the bag tip down in a tall drinking glass and fold the top edges of the bag around the perimeter of the glass to hold it up.

5. Fill the bag with the melted chocolate. Take the filled bag out of the glass and twist the top to prevent leakage.

6. Squeeze little chocolate teardrops onto the parchment paper until the bag is empty.

7. Place the cookie sheet in the freezer until the chips harden, about 1 hour.

Store the chocolate chips in the freezer, in an airtight plastic bag or freezer-safe glass jar, until you're ready to bake with them.

ALL-PURPOSE GLUTEN-FREE FLOUR MIX

This is the mix you'll make as the basis for every recipe in this book. You should double or triple the recipe so you have a nice big batch at the ready whenever you need it. In order to save money, you can buy all these flours in bulk and store them in an airtight container in the freezer. This will extend their shelf life for up to a year.

MUST HAVE

1 cup tapioca flour
¾ cup sorghum flour
¾ cup millet flour
¼ cup ivory teff flour
¼ cup quinoa flour

MUST DO

1. Put all the flours in a gallon-size ziplock Baggie and toss it around and turn it upside down to thoroughly combine.

When measuring out gluten-free flour for a recipe, always loosen it up first by shaking its container, whether it be a tub of Tupperware or the aforementioned ziplock. Then scoop it up with a large spoon and transfer it into the measuring cup and level it off. You have to do it this way because gluten-free flour is very dense and compact, and you don't want to end up with more volume in your measuring cup than is called for in the recipe.

Tool Kit

Here is a list of the essentials you need for baking with this book.

Big Spoon or Whisk
Either will do for stirring and mixing. You won't need a hand mixer or a stand-up mixer for any of these recipes.

Espresso Spoon
When you decorate your goodies with swirls of frosting, use this darling utensil.

Baking Spatula
The head of a baking spatula should be rubber or silicone. You'll use this for smoothing out batters evenly in the pan.

Stainless-Steel Slotted Spatula
This spatula is used for lifting delicate cookies and brownies from the pan and rescuing dough balls from drowning in baking-soda baths.

Measuring Spoons
Make sure yours are stainless-steel, as they last the longest. Also, make sure your measuring spoon set includes a ⅛ teaspoon. You'll be using that one a lot.

Measuring Cups
You'll need one measuring cup that holds at least 2 cups for mixing ingredients and microwaving. I use a glass measuring cup for this purpose.

You'll need stainless-steel measuring cups that include 1, ½, ⅓ and ¼ cups to measure both dry and liquid ingredients for these recipes.

Mixing Bowls

You'll need a large stainless-steel mixing bowl and a medium-size one for mixing ingredients. You'll also need a medium-size and small microwave-safe bowl for making sauces, glazes and frostings.

8 x 8 x 2-inch Aluminum Baking Pan

You'll use this pan for baking brownies, quick breads and energy bars.

15 x 10 x 1-inch Aluminum Jelly-Roll Pan

You'll use this pan for baking energy bars and donut holes.

15 x 13-inch Aluminum Cookie or Baking Sheet

With its curled-up edges on the short sides and flat edges on the long sides, this sheet is indispensible for baking cookies and breads.

Standard 12-Cup Muffin Tin

This muffin tin has wells for twelve standard-size muffins. The wells are an inch bigger than those of a cupcake tin. You'll also need this muffin tin for some of the bread roll recipes.

Standard 12-Cup Cupcake Tin

This cupcake tin has wells for twelve standard-size cupcakes.

24-Cup Mini Muffin Tin

This muffin tin has twenty-four wells and is used for some of the mini recipes in this book. Surprisingly, you won't need it for mini muffins or cupcakes, but rather petite brownies and breads.

Standard-Size and Mini Paper Baking Cups

Paper baking cups are essential to prevent sticking and to avoid messy cleanups when making the muffins and cupcakes and some of the miniature brownies and breads in this book.

Biscuit Cutter
A biscuit cutter allows you to make circles that are the perfect size for the pizza wheels.

Parchment Paper
Parchment paper works wonders to prevent sticky situations when baking. Wax paper does not.

Wire Cooling Racks
These are needed for the proper cooling down of baked goods when they come out of the oven.

Cutting Board
A cutting board is necessary for chopping fruits, vegetables and potatoes.

Steamer
A steamer is used to cook and soften up vegetables when preparing purees.

Potato Ricer
You'll need one of these to make perfectly smooth purees.

Coffee Grinder
A coffee grinder provides an easy way to grind seeds and grains.

Food Processor or High-Speed Blender
These tools are sometimes used when making purees and combining ingredients.

CHAPTER 3

POWER MUFFINS

First thing in the morning, my son has to have one of these grand-slam breakfast muffins, and I need my coffee so no one gets hurt. And since he never used to eat anything wholesome that wasn't already baked into a tortilla chip, I have found these muffins to be my savior.

I find that the more compact a food item, the easier and faster it is to get out the door at the start of the day. So each power muffin is packed to capacity with nutrition. Beginning with a live-wire flour base and ending with energy-boosting fats and fruits that are bursting with flavor, these dynamos are so stuffed with vitamins, minerals and roughage, it is standing room only in there. And the best part about it is these morning glories will get those little butts out of bed with absolutely no fuss at all.

MUSHY MONKEY BANANA MUFFINS

Makes 12 standard-size muffins

There is something very comforting and curious about these banana muffins. It must have something to do with Curious George (which my son watches ad nauseam), because once they cool on the rack, he hoards them and sleeps with them under his pillow so he can have breakfast in bed. This is where the "mushy" comes from. And I blame the oddball monkey. I'm sure he's responsible. In any event, these potassium-rich muffins have the added benefit of turmeric, a spice that has wonderful anti-inflammatory and antibacterial properties, as well as a mellow yellow hat . . . I mean hue.

MUST HAVE

12 standard-size paper baking cups
2 cups all-purpose gluten-free flour (see page 13)
2 teaspoons sodium-free baking powder
1 teaspoon baking soda
½ teaspoon guar gum
¼ teaspoon fine sea salt
¼ cup grapeseed oil
¼ cup coconut nectar
½ teaspoon turmeric powder
⅜ teaspoon stevia powder
1 cup mashed banana (about 2 large bananas)
¾ cup unsweetened plain rice milk

MUST DO

1. Preheat oven to 350°F. Line a standard 12-cup muffin tin with paper baking cups.

2. Whisk together the flour, baking powder, baking soda, guar gum and salt in a large bowl. Make a well in the middle.

3. Add the grapeseed oil, coconut nectar, turmeric powder and stevia and stir to combine. Add the mashed banana and rice milk, and stir until the liquid is absorbed and the batter is smooth.

4. Spoon the batter into the prepared muffin tin, dividing it evenly. Each cup should be about three-quarters full.

5. Bake the muffins for 18 to 20 minutes, or until they are a light golden brown and bounce back slightly to the touch. Rotate the muffin tin from front to back halfway through baking.

6. Transfer the muffin tin from the oven to a wire rack and let sit for 10 minutes before removing the muffins to cool completely.

Keep muffins in an airtight container for up to 3 days, or wrap and freeze for up to 3 months.

Nutrition Information Per Serving (1 muffin): 150 calories, 5 g total fat, 0.0 mg cholesterol, 23 g carbohydrates, 160 mg sodium, 2 g fiber, 2 g protein, 6 g sugars

PUMPKIN PIE MUFFINS

Makes 12 standard-size muffins

Pumpkin isn't just your Fall guy anymore. Mr. Pumpkin is now available all year round in all his orange eminence. He is rich in beta-carotene, vitamins C and E, magnesium and potassium. And pumpkin pie spice, a premixed blend of cinnamon, ginger, lemon peel, nutmeg, cloves and cardamom, found in any grocery store, is a potent potpourri that has healing anti-inflammatory and antioxidant benefits. So, I beg of you, don't wait for October, November or December before you whip up these muffs, because passion for pumpkin is not seasonal anymore.

MUST HAVE

Muffins

12 standard-size paper baking cups
2 cups all-purpose gluten-free flour (see page 13)
1 tablespoon pumpkin pie spice
2 teaspoons sodium-free baking powder
1 teaspoon baking soda
½ teaspoon guar gum
¼ teaspoon fine sea salt
¼ cup grapeseed oil
¼ cup coconut nectar
⅜ teaspoon stevia powder
1 cup canned pumpkin puree
¾ cup unsweetened plain rice milk

Topping

2 teaspoons cinnamon powder

MUST DO

1. Preheat oven to 350°F. Line a standard 12-cup muffin tin with paper baking cups.

2. Whisk together the flour, pumpkin pie spice, baking powder, baking soda, guar gum and salt in a large bowl. Make a well in the middle.

3. Add the grapeseed oil, coconut nectar and stevia and stir to combine. Add the pumpkin puree and rice milk, and stir until the liquid is absorbed and the batter is smooth.

4. Spoon the batter into the prepared muffin tin, dividing it evenly. Each cup should be about three-quarters full. Dust the top of each with a sprinkling of cinnamon.

5. Bake the muffins for 16 to 18 minutes, or until they are golden orange and bounce back slightly to the touch. Rotate the muffin tin from front to back halfway through baking.

6. Transfer the muffin tin from the oven to a wire rack and let sit for about 10 minutes before removing the muffins to cool completely.

Keep in an airtight container for up to 3 days, or wrap and freeze for up to 3 months.

Nutrition Information Per Serving (1 muffin): 150 calories, 5 g total fat, 0.0 mg cholesterol, 24 g carbohydrates, 160 mg sodium, 3 g fiber, 2 g protein, 4 g sugars

SALTED CARAMEL APPLE MUFFINS

Makes 12 standard-size muffins

If I had to choose one candy I miss most since giving up dairy and refined sugar, it would have to be caramels. There is something about their chewy, sweet gooeyness that is very comforting (and cavity inducing). So imagine my ecstasy when I tasted my fake caramel sauce for this recipe for the first time. It is so good that it instantly became my friend and faux simultaneously. Make this for people you love, because they will take a pledge of allegiance to you forever.

MUST HAVE

Muffins

12 standard-size paper baking cups

2 cups all-purpose gluten-free flour (see page 13)

2 teaspoons sodium-free baking powder

1 teaspoon baking soda

1 teaspoon cinnamon powder

½ teaspoon guar gum

¼ teaspoon fine sea salt

¼ cup grapeseed oil

¼ cup coconut nectar

¼ teaspoon stevia powder

¾ cup unsweetened plain rice milk

½ cup unsweetened applesauce

1 small Gala or Granny Smith apple (about 5 ounces), peeled, cored and sliced into ¼-inch pieces

Caramel Sauce

½ cup coconut nectar

¼ cup sunflower seed butter (see page 11)

⅛ teaspoon fine sea salt

MUST DO

1. Preheat oven to 350°F. Line a standard 12-cup muffin tin with paper baking cups.

2. To make the muffins, whisk together the flour, baking powder, baking soda, cinnamon, guar gum and salt in a large bowl. Make a well in the middle.

3. Add the grapeseed oil, coconut nectar and stevia and stir to combine. Add the rice milk and applesauce, and stir until the liquid is absorbed and the batter is smooth.

4. Fold in about half of the apple pieces.

5. To make the caramel sauce, mix together the coconut nectar, sunflower seed butter and salt in a small bowl until well blended.

6. Spoon the batter into the prepared muffin tin, dividing it evenly. Each cup should be about two-thirds full. Top each with the caramel sauce and the remaining apple pieces.

7. Bake the muffins for 16 to 18 minutes, or until they are a light golden brown and bounce back slightly to the touch. Rotate the muffin tin from front to back halfway through baking.

8. Transfer the muffin tin from the oven to a wire rack and let rest for about 10 minutes before removing the muffins to cool completely.

Keep in an airtight container for up to 3 days, or wrap and freeze for up to 3 months.

Nutrition Information Per Serving (1 muffin): 170 calories, 6 g total fat, 0.0 mg cholesterol, 27 g carbohydrates, 170 mg sodium, 2 g fiber, 3 g protein, 11 g sugars

SUNFLOWER BUTTER AND JELLY MUFFINS

Makes 12 standard-size muffins

Little Miss Sunflower Seed is like an A-list movie star because she contains elusive, hard-to-get selenium, which, among other wondrous things, is involved in reproductive health for men. Selenium is a trace mineral that possesses extremely powerful antioxidant properties, which help your body rebel against disease. So get ready for your close-up, Miss Seedy, because you have the lead role in this jelly roll.

MUST HAVE

12 standard-size paper baking cups

2 cups all-purpose gluten-free flour (see page 13)

2 teaspoons sodium-free baking powder

1 teaspoon baking soda

½ teaspoon guar gum

¼ teaspoon fine sea salt

¼ cup grapeseed oil

3 tablespoons coconut nectar

⅜ teaspoon stevia powder

½ cup grape jelly

½ cup sunflower seed butter (see page 11)

1 cup unsweetened plain rice milk

MUST DO

1. Preheat oven to 350°F. Line a standard 12-cup muffin tin with paper baking cups.

2. Whisk together the flour, baking powder, baking soda, guar gum and salt in a large bowl. Make a well in the middle.

3. Add the grapeseed oil, coconut nectar and stevia and stir to combine. Add the grape jelly, sunflower seed butter and rice milk and stir until the liquid is absorbed.

4. Spoon the batter into the prepared muffin tin, dividing it evenly. Each cup should be about three-quarters full.

5. Bake the muffins for 15 to 17 minutes, or until they are a light golden brown and bounce back slightly to the touch. Rotate the muffin tin from front to back halfway through baking.

6. Transfer the muffin tin from the oven to a wire rack and let sit for 10 minutes before removing the muffins to cool completely.

Keep in an airtight container for up to 3 days, or wrap and freeze for up to 3 months.

Nutrition Information Per Serving (1 muffin): 210 calories, 10 g total fat, 0.0 mg cholesterol, 28 g carbohydrates, 170 mg sodium, 2 g fiber, 3 g protein, 4 g sugars

Sweet Truth:

You can use the plum lemon jam from the Plum Lemon Pinkyprints recipe (see page 61) as a substitute for the grape jelly with equally magnificent results.

STONED FRUIT MUFFINS

Makes 12 standard-size muffins

Even though I don't have one yet, I remember being one, and I truly believe that teenagers are the reason Moms become premature antiques. If I remember correctly, it is at this age that children grow an appendage called "attitude," because they know way, way more than you. So just save your breath and tell your kid what you've made them for breakfast, because I'm sure their ears will perk up when you tell them you've made them muffins with stoned fruit.

MUST HAVE

12 standard-size paper baking cups

2 cups all-purpose gluten-free flour (see page 13)

2 teaspoons sodium-free baking powder

1 teaspoon baking soda

¾ teaspoon ginger powder

½ teaspoon guar gum

¼ teaspoon ground cardamom

¼ teaspoon fine sea salt

¼ cup grapeseed oil

¼ cup coconut nectar

¼ teaspoon stevia powder

1 cup unsweetened plain rice milk

⅓ cup apricot, peach, nectarine or plum puree

1 cup diced apricots, peaches, nectarines or plums

MUST DO

1. Preheat oven to 350°F. Line a standard 12-cup muffin tin with paper baking cups.

2. Whisk together the flour, baking powder, baking soda, ginger, guar gum, cardamom and salt in a large bowl. Make a well in the middle.

3. Add the grapeseed oil, coconut nectar and stevia and stir to combine. Add the rice milk and fruit puree, and stir until the liquid is absorbed and the batter is smooth.

4. Add ½ cup of the diced fruit and stir to distribute evenly.

5. Spoon the batter into the prepared muffin tin, dividing it evenly. Each cup should be about two-thirds full. Top each with the remaining ½ cup of diced fruit.

6. Bake the muffins for 17 to 18 minutes, or until they are a light golden brown and bounce back slightly to the touch. Rotate the muffin tin from front to back halfway through baking.

7. Transfer the muffin tin from the oven to a wire rack and let sit for 10 minutes before removing the muffins to cool completely.

Keep in an airtight container for up to 3 days, or wrap and freeze for up to 3 months.

Nutrition Information Per Serving (1 muffin): 150 calories, 5 g total fat, 0.0 mg cholesterol, 26 g carbohydrates, 160 mg sodium, 2 g fiber, 2 g protein, 5 g sugars

---

CRAN BAN THANK YOU BRAN MUFFINS

Makes 12 standard-size muffins

When I was about eight weeks pregnant, my husband started to smell bad. I didn't realize at the time that my warped sense of smell was a result of a tsunami of hormones invading my body, not a change in my husband's. This was followed by an ambush of nausea and strange cravings. Then, in a cruel turn of events, my plumbing got plugged up. When your digestive system is acting so unprofessionally, it's important to have an edible intervention, pregnant or not pregnant. Bran is definitely famous for its fiber. Cranberries and bananas, not so much. But, in addition to an abundance of potassium and antioxidants, cranberries and bananas pack a fibrous punch. Roughage aside, the combination of the tangy cranberry, mellow banana and crispy bran makes this the mother of all muffins.

MUST HAVE

12 standard-size paper baking cups

1 cup rice bran

1¼ cups unsweetened plain rice milk

¼ cup mashed banana

1 cup all-purpose gluten-free flour (see page 13)

2 teaspoons cinnamon powder

2 teaspoons sodium-free baking powder

1 teaspoon baking soda

½ teaspoon guar gum

¼ teaspoon fine sea salt

¼ cup grapeseed oil

¼ cup coconut nectar

¼ teaspoon stevia powder

¼ cup water

¾ cup dried cranberries

MUST DO

1. Preheat oven to 350°F. Line a standard 12-cup muffin tin with paper baking cups.

2. Place the rice bran in a medium-size bowl. Add the rice milk and stir until well blended and absorbed. Fold in the mashed banana.

3. In a large bowl, whisk together the flour, cinnamon, baking powder, baking soda, guar gum and salt. Make a well in the middle.

4. Add the grapeseed oil, coconut nectar, stevia and water to the dry ingredients, and stir until the liquid is absorbed and the batter is smooth. Next add the rice bran mixture and stir to combine. Add ½ cup of the dried cranberries and stir to distribute evenly.

5. Spoon the batter into the prepared muffin tin, dividing it evenly. Each cup should

be about two-thirds full. Top each with the remaining ¼ cup of dried cranberries.

6. Bake the muffins for 18 to 20 minutes, or until they are a light golden brown and bounce back slightly to the touch. Rotate the muffin tin from front to back halfway through baking.

7. Transfer the muffin tin from the oven to a wire rack and let sit for 10 minutes before removing the muffins to cool completely.

Keep in an airtight container for up to 3 days, or wrap individually and freeze for up to 3 months.

Nutrition Information Per Serving (1 muffin):
160 calories, 6 g total fat, 0.0 mg cholesterol,
25 g carbohydrates, 160 mg sodium, 3 g fiber,
2 g protein, 9 g sugars

DILLICIOUS HERB-STUFFED MUFFINS

Makes 12 standard-size muffins

And now for something completely different, a savory muffin with all the most vibrant herbs your spice rack or garden can hold. My favorite is dill. Its fragrance and flavor enhance any dish. And with the additions of rosemary, thyme and oregano, this muffin smacks of a garden Alice Waters might have planted. Maybe you and your kids can plant these herbs in the backyard and have them at your fingertips whenever you feel the urge to have a Dillicious Muffin.

MUST HAVE

Muffins

12 standard-size paper baking cups

1 small cauliflower (about 12 ounces), divided into small florets

1 cup unsweetened plain rice milk

1 teaspoon apple cider vinegar

2 cups all-purpose gluten-free flour (see page 13)

6 teaspoons minced fresh dill, or 3 teaspoons dried dill

2 teaspoons finely minced fresh rosemary, or 1 teaspoon dried rosemary

2 teaspoons dried thyme

2 teaspoons dried minced onion

2 teaspoons sodium-free baking powder

1 teaspoon baking soda

1 teaspoon dried oregano

½ teaspoon guar gum

½ teaspoon chili powder (optional)

½ teaspoon fine sea salt

¼ cup grapeseed oil

¾ cup shredded vegan, soy-free cheddar cheese (I use Daiya cheddar cheese. See resources for more information.)

Topping

1 tablespoon dried dill

MUST DO

1. Preheat oven to 350°F. Line a standard 12-cup muffin tin with paper baking cups.

2. Steam the cauliflower florets in a medium-size saucepan for about 15 minutes, or until tender. Transfer the florets, a few at a time, to a potato ricer and push them through into a medium-size bowl. This will give you lumpless cauliflower puree.

3. Mix together the rice milk and vinegar in a 2-cup measuring cup.

4. Whisk together the flour, dill, rosemary, thyme, minced onion, baking powder, baking soda, oregano, guar gum, chili powder, if using, and salt in a large bowl. Make a well in the middle.

5. Add the cauliflower puree, rice milk mixture and grapeseed oil, and stir until the liquid is absorbed and the batter is smooth. Fold in ½ cup of the cheddar cheese.

6. Spoon the batter into the prepared muffin tin, dividing it evenly. Each cup should be about three-quarters full. Top each with the remaining ¼ cup of cheese. Dust the top of each with a sprinkling of dill.

7. Bake the muffins for 18 to 20 minutes, or until they are a light golden brown and bounce back slightly to the touch. Rotate the muffin tin from front to back halfway through baking.

8. Transfer the muffin tin from the oven to a wire rack and let sit for 10 minutes before removing the muffins to cool completely.

Keep in an airtight container for up to 3 days, or wrap and freeze for up to 3 months.

Nutrition Information Per Serving (1 muffin): 140 calories, 6 g total fat, 0.0 mg cholesterol, 25 g carbohydrates, 185 mg sodium, 3 g fiber, 2 g protein, 1 g sugars

---

MANGO BUCKWHEAT PANCAKE MUFFINS

Makes 12 standard-size muffins

If you had to choose which of the muffins in this chapter to give your kids right before school, it should be this one. In recent studies, mango has been found to help children concentrate and to increase memory retention due to its glutamine acid content. Also, mango contains enzymes that are helpful in digestion, as well as soluble dietary fiber and antioxidants. And best of all, when your teenager's face breaks out with acne, you can put these muffins on his or her face, because mango helps clear clogged pores. Just a serving suggestion.

MUST HAVE

12 standard-size paper baking cups
1¼ cups all-purpose gluten-free flour (see page 13)
¾ cup light buckwheat flour
2 teaspoons sodium-free baking powder
2 teaspoons ginger powder
1 teaspoon baking soda
1 teaspoon cinnamon powder
½ teaspoon guar gum
¼ teaspoon fine sea salt
¼ cup grapeseed oil
¼ cup coconut nectar
¼ teaspoon stevia powder
¾ cup unsweetened plain rice milk
½ cup fresh or frozen (thawed) mango puree
½ cup fresh or frozen (thawed) mango, cut into ¼-inch dice

MUST DO

1. Preheat oven to 350°F. Line a standard 12-cup muffin tin with paper baking cups.

2. Whisk together the two flours, baking powder, ginger, baking soda, cinnamon, guar gum and salt in a large bowl. Make a well in the middle.

3. Add the grapeseed oil, coconut nectar and stevia and stir to combine. Add the rice milk and mango puree, and stir until the liquid is absorbed and the batter is smooth.

4. Spoon the batter into the prepared muffin tin, dividing it evenly. Each cup should be about two-thirds full. Top each with a sprinkling of the diced mango.

5. Bake the muffins for 18 to 20 minutes, or until they are a light golden brown and bounce back slightly to the touch. Rotate the muffin tin from front to back halfway through baking.

6. Transfer the muffin tin from the oven to a wire rack and let sit for 10 minutes before removing the muffins to cool completely.

Keep in an airtight container for up to 3 days, or wrap and freeze for up to 3 months.

Nutrition Information Per Serving (1 muffin): 150 calories, 5 g total fat, 0.0 mg cholesterol, 25 g carbohydrates, 160 mg sodium, 2 g fiber, 2 g protein, 6 g sugars

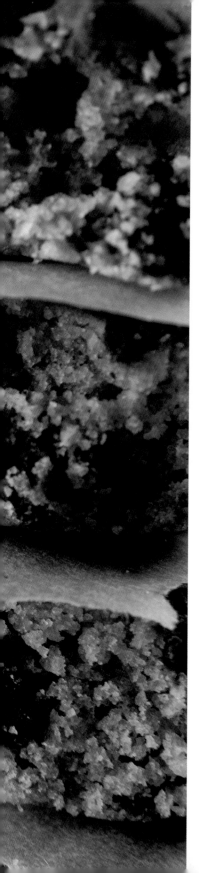

CHAPTER 4

BROWNIE POINTS

The good thing about brownies is they love to dress up and accessorize. Just accent them with superfoods, like mesquite and green tea, and spices, such as cayenne, and then top them with a tasteful frosting, and they're ready to go out in their red high heels and party.

If you like your brownies a little underdone, like I prefer them, go for the lower bake time suggested and you will experience a melt-in-your-mouth, otherworldly fudge-like creation. If you want to take it one step further, put the brownies in the freezer overnight, and then eat two squares and thank me in the morning.

GOURMET DARK CHOCOLATE MESQUITE BROWNIES

Makes 16 brownies

Mesquite powder is a nutritionally dense, gluten-free flour that exudes the flavors of caramel, chocolate and molasses. It is exceptionally high in calcium, potassium, iron, zinc and the amino acid lysine, and it helps even out blood sugar levels over an extended period of time. You can find it very easily online or in health food stores. But beware. When mesquite powder gets into bed with other gluten-free flours, flavorful fireworks ignite. Maybe that's why they named grills after it.

MUST HAVE

Brownies

Grapeseed oil, for greasing the pan

1 cup all-purpose gluten-free flour (see page 13)

½ cup cacao powder

2 tablespoons mesquite powder

½ teaspoon baking soda

½ teaspoon guar gum

¼ teaspoon fine sea salt

7 tablespoons grapeseed oil

5 tablespoons coconut nectar

2 teaspoons vanilla extract

⅜ teaspoon stevia powder

½ cup water

Chocolate Frosting

3 tablespoons coconut oil

2 tablespoons coconut nectar

¼ cup powdered erythritol

3 tablespoons cacao powder

½ tablespoon warm water

⅛ teaspoon stevia powder

⅛ teaspoon fine sea salt

MUST DO

1. Preheat oven to 325°F. Grease an 8 x 8-inch square baking pan with grapeseed oil.

2. To make the brownies, whisk together the flour, cacao powder, mesquite powder, baking soda, guar gum and salt in a large bowl. Make a well in the middle.

3. Add the grapeseed oil, coconut nectar, vanilla and stevia and stir to combine. Next add the water and stir until it is absorbed and the batter is smooth.

4. Spoon the batter into the prepared pan and smooth down with a wet baking spatula or the back of a wet spoon.

5. Bake the brownies for 11 to 12 minutes, or until the batter starts to pull away from the sides of the pan and a toothpick inserted in the center comes out with just a few crumbs attached. Rotate the pan from front to back after 9 minutes of baking.

6. Transfer the pan from the oven to a wire rack and let sit for about 30 minutes before cutting the brownies into 16 squares.

7. To make the frosting, mix together the coconut oil and coconut nectar in a small bowl. Add the powdered erythritol, cacao powder, warm water, stevia and salt and stir until smooth and well combined.

8. Frost the brownies when they are completely cool.

Keep in an airtight container for up to 3 days, or wrap and freeze for up to 3 months.

Nutrition Information Per Serving (1 brownie): 130 calories, 8 g total fat, 0.0 mg cholesterol, 16 g carbohydrates, 80 mg sodium, 1 g fiber, 1 g protein, 6 g sugars

---

Sweet Truth:

Please be sure to wait for the brownies to cool completely, or they will fall apart when you try to cut them.

LEMON PARSNIPANNIES

Makes 16 parsnipannies

I didn't plan on naming these brownies after a similar-sounding township in New Jersey; it just baked out that way. Once I realized that a pureed parsnip adds a luxurious scrumptiousness to brownies that is hard to describe, I started to tremble with excitement at the possibilities. This funny-looking albino root vegetable is a great source of vitamins B_6, C and E, as well as folic acid, magnesium and niacin. And the pairing of parsnip and lemon is serendipitous.

MUST HAVE

Parsnipannies

Coconut oil, for greasing the pan

1 small parsnip (about 4 ounces)

1½ cups all-purpose gluten-free flour (see page 13)

1 teaspoon sodium-free baking powder

⅜ teaspoon guar gum

¼ teaspoon baking soda

¼ teaspoon ground nutmeg

¼ teaspoon fine sea salt

¼ cup coconut oil

2 tablespoons coconut nectar

2 tablespoons freshly squeezed lemon juice

1 teaspoon lemon extract

⅜ teaspoon stevia powder

½ cup unsweetened coconut milk

Lemon Icing

1 tablespoon coconut nectar

1 tablespoon coconut oil

1 cup powdered erythritol

3 tablespoons freshly squeezed lemon juice

⅛ teaspoon turmeric powder

⅛ teaspoon fine sea salt

MUST DO

1. Preheat oven to 325°F. Grease an 8 x 8-inch square baking pan with coconut oil.

2. Peel the skin off the parsnip and slice it into ½-inch-thick pieces. Steam the parsnip pieces in a medium-size saucepan for about 15 minutes, or until tender. Transfer the parsnip pieces to a potato ricer and push them through into a small bowl. This will give you lumpless parsnip puree. Measure out ⅓ cup of the puree and set aside.

3. To make the parsnipannies, whisk together the flour, baking powder, guar gum, baking soda, nutmeg and salt in a large bowl. Make a well in the middle.

4. Microwave the coconut oil and coconut nectar in a 2-cup measuring cup for 20 seconds. Add the lemon juice, lemon extract and stevia and stir to combine. Pour into the flour mixture.

5. Next add the parsnip puree and coconut milk to the flour mixture, and stir until the liquid is absorbed and the batter is smooth.

6. Spoon the batter into the prepared pan and smooth down with a wet baking spatula or the back of a wet spoon.

7. Bake the parsnipannies for 13 to 15 minutes, or until the batter is a light golden brown and starts to pull away from the sides of the pan. Rotate the pan from front to back after about 9 minutes of baking.

8. Transfer the pan from the oven to a wire rack and let sit for about 20 minutes before cutting the parsnipannies into 16 squares.

9. **To make the lemon icing**, microwave the coconut nectar and coconut oil in a medium-size microwave-safe bowl for 20 seconds. Add the powdered erythritol, lemon juice, turmeric powder and salt and stir until smooth and well combined.

10. When the parsnipannies are completely cool, top each with icing.

Keep in an airtight container for up to 3 days, or wrap and freeze for up to 3 months.

Nutrition Information Per Serving (1 parsnipanny): 150 calories, 10 g total fat, 0.0 mg cholesterol, 14 g carbohydrates, 80 mg sodium, 2 g fiber, 1 g protein, 6 g sugars

Sweet Truth:

You can serve any leftover parsnip puree as a healthy snack or as a side dish in place of mashed potatoes. Add some tasty herbs and spices from your garden and spice rack, and I guarantee a standing ovation from your dining audience.

GIRL SCOUT BROWNIES

Makes 16 brownies

One of the world's most beloved Girl Scout cookies is Samoas. Of course, those delicious cookies are filled with allergens, not to mention hydrogenated fats and sugar. So to bring some semblance of wholesomeness to this longtime fave, I re-created the cookie's delicious romance of vanilla cake with toasted coconut and caramel, all drizzled silly with dark chocolate sauce, and reincarnated it as a brownie. It'll sweep you off your feet, it's that good. Scout's honor! (Or is that for the boys?)

MUST HAVE

Topping

3 tablespoons unsweetened shredded coconut

Caramel Sauce

½ cup coconut nectar

¼ cup sunflower seed butter (see page 11)

¼ teaspoon fine sea salt

Chocolate Sauce

1 tablespoon coconut oil

1 tablespoon coconut nectar

2 tablespoons cacao powder

⅛ teaspoon stevia powder

⅛ teaspoon fine sea salt

Brownies

Coconut oil, for greasing the pan

1¾ cups all-purpose gluten-free flour (see page 13)

¾ teaspoon sodium-free baking powder

⅜ teaspoon guar gum

¼ teaspoon baking soda

¼ teaspoon fine sea salt

¼ cup coconut oil

3 tablespoons coconut nectar

½ cup unsweetened coconut milk

¼ cup warm water

2 teaspoons vanilla extract

¼ teaspoon stevia powder

MUST DO

1. **To make the topping,** spread the shredded coconut in a small frying pan and toast for about 10 minutes over medium heat. Stir the coconut halfway through to ensure even toasting.

2. **To make the caramel sauce,** mix together the coconut nectar, sunflower seed butter and salt in a small bowl until well combined.

3. **To make the chocolate sauce,** microwave the coconut oil and coconut nectar in a small microwave-safe bowl for 20 seconds. Add the cacao powder, stevia and salt and stir until smooth and well combined.

4. Preheat oven to 325°F. Grease an 8 x 8-inch square baking pan with coconut oil.

5. **To make the brownies,** whisk together the flour, baking powder, guar gum, baking soda and salt in a large bowl. Make a well in the middle.

6. Microwave the coconut oil and coconut nectar in a measuring cup for 20 seconds. Add the coconut milk, warm water, vanilla and stevia and stir to combine. Pour into the flour mixture and stir until the liquid is absorbed and the batter is smooth.

7. Spoon the batter into the prepared pan and smooth down with a wet baking spatula or the back of a wet spoon.

8. Spread the caramel sauce evenly over the batter and top with the toasted coconut. Drizzle the chocolate sauce over the caramel and coconut.

9. Bake the brownies for 15 to 17 minutes, or until the batter starts to pull away from the sides of the pan and a toothpick inserted in the center comes out with just a few crumbs attached. Rotate the pan halfway through baking.

10. Transfer the pan from the oven to a wire rack and let sit for about 15 minutes before cutting the brownies into 16 squares.

Keep in an airtight container for up to 3 days, or wrap and freeze for up to 3 months.

Nutrition Information Per Serving (1 brownie): 200 calories, 14 g total fat, 0.0 mg cholesterol, 21 g carbohydrates, 77 mg sodium, 1 g fiber, 2 g protein, 9 g sugars

Sweet Truth:

Freeze these for brownies that taste like English toffee.

UNMATCHABLE MATCHA TEANIES

Makes 24 mini-muffin-size teanies

These are the perfect accompaniment to a tea party of any size. Whether it's high tea at three o'clock for the ladies or a tea party for your budding princesses, these teanies add unparalleled nutritional perks. In addition to vitamin C, chromium, zinc and magnesium, Matcha green tea contains unique and powerful antioxidants called catechins, which counteract the effect of free radicals, a cause of DNA damage. I also add hemp seeds to the batter and the frosting to bump up the protein, omega-3, omega-6 and phytonutrient content. Just some added health insurance.

MUST HAVE

Teanies

24 mini paper baking cups

2½ cups all-purpose gluten-free flour (see page 13)

2 teaspoons Matcha green tea powder

1 teaspoon sodium-free baking powder

¾ teaspoon baking soda

¾ teaspoon guar gum

½ teaspoon fine sea salt

¼ teaspoon coriander powder

½ cup grapeseed oil

⅓ cup coconut nectar

2 teaspoons vanilla extract

⅜ teaspoon stevia powder

¾ cup water

¼ cup unsweetened plain rice milk

⅓ cup hemp seeds

Frosting

1 cup hemp seed butter (see page 10)

¼ cup coconut nectar

⅛ teaspoon Matcha green tea powder

⅛ teaspoon fine sea salt

MUST DO

1. Preheat oven to 325°F. Line a 24-cup mini muffin tin with mini paper baking cups.

2. **To make the teanies**, whisk together the flour, Matcha green tea powder, baking powder, baking soda, guar gum, salt and coriander in a large bowl. Make a well in the middle.

3. Add the grapeseed oil, coconut nectar, vanilla and stevia and stir to combine. Next add the water and rice milk, and stir until the liquid is absorbed and the batter is smooth. Stir in the hemp seeds and mix well to distribute evenly.

4. Spoon the batter into the prepared muffin tin, filling the cups to the top.

5. Bake the teanies for 13 to 14 minutes, or until they are a light golden brown around the edges and bounce back slightly to the touch. Rotate the muffin tin from front to back after 10 minutes of baking.

6. Transfer the muffin tin from the oven to a wire rack and let sit for about 15 minutes before removing the teanies to cool completely.

7. **To make the frosting**, mix together the hemp seed butter, coconut nectar, Matcha green tea powder and salt in a small bowl and stir to combine.

8. Frost the teanies when they are completely cool.

Keep in an airtight container for up to 3 days, or wrap and freeze for up to 3 months.

———◇———

Nutrition Information Per Serving (1 teanie):
180 calories, 8 g total fat, 0.0 mg cholesterol,
16 g carbohydrates, 80 mg sodium, 2 g fiber,
3 g protein, 7 g sugars

———◇———

BLONDIES WITH ROOTS

Makes 16 blondies

If you highlight your locks, like I used to do, you will especially appreciate this platinum pixie snack with its chic chocolate chip roots and sophisticated spices of coriander and cardamom. Cardamom is rich in vitamin C and riboflavin, and is considered beneficial to the kidneys and bladder. Coriander is high in potassium and calcium, as well, and aids in digestion. And after your first bite, I'm sure you'll agree that blondies are more fun!

MUST HAVE

Grapeseed oil, for greasing the pan
1½ cups all-purpose gluten-free flour (see page 13)
¾ teaspoon sodium-free baking powder
¼ teaspoon coriander powder
¼ teaspoon ground cardamom
¼ teaspoon baking soda
¼ teaspoon guar gum
¼ teaspoon fine sea salt
½ cup unsweetened plain rice milk
¼ cup grapeseed oil
¼ cup coconut nectar
2 teaspoons vanilla extract
¼ teaspoon stevia powder
1 cup chocolate chips (see page 12)

MUST DO

1. Preheat oven to 325°F. Grease an 8 x 8-inch square baking pan with grapeseed oil.

2. Whisk together the flour, baking powder, coriander, cardamom, baking soda, guar gum and salt in a large bowl. Make a well in the middle.

3. Add the rice milk, grapeseed oil, coconut nectar, vanilla and stevia and stir to combine. Fold in ¾ cup of the chocolate chips.

4. Spoon the batter into the prepared pan and smooth down with a wet baking spatula or the back of a wet spoon. Top with the remaining ¼ cup of chocolate chips.

5. Bake the blondies for 15 to 16 minutes, or until the batter turns a light golden brown and starts to pull away from the sides of the pan. Rotate the pan halfway through baking.

6. Transfer the pan from the oven to a wire rack and let sit for about 20 minutes before cutting the blondies into 16 squares.

Keep in an airtight container for up to 3 days, or wrap and freeze for up to 3 months.

Nutrition Information Per Serving (1 blondie): 110 calories, 5 g total fat, 0.0 mg cholesterol, 15 g carbohydrates, 60 mg sodium, 1 g fiber, 1 g protein, 5 g sugars

SUNFLOWER BUTTERCUP BROWNIES

Makes 24 mini-muffin-size buttercups

The most traumatic moment of my childhood was when I realized that peanut butter cups were a seasonal food. They don't do well in the hot summer months, and they were banned from the tote when we went to Jones Beach. When I first set out to create these brownies, I vowed that they would be my little peanut buttercup perennials. What I got was so much more. The sunflower seed butter caramelizes with the chocolate, and the brownies have a butter-like aroma when they come out of the oven. It may be un-American to say this, but these buttercups rival the original, and my kid eats them at the ballpark, in bed (see the Mushy Monkey Banana Muffins story) and even on the shores of Los Angeles.

MUST HAVE

24 mini paper baking cups
2 cups all-purpose gluten-free flour (see page 13)
2½ teaspoons sodium-free baking powder
½ teaspoon guar gum
½ teaspoon fine sea salt
½ cup grapeseed oil
½ cup unsweetened applesauce
⅓ cup coconut nectar
1 teaspoon vanilla extract
⅜ teaspoon stevia powder
1 cup sunflower seed butter (see page 11)
1¼ cups chocolate chips (see page 12)

MUST DO

1. Preheat oven to 325°F. Line a 24-cup mini muffin tin with mini paper baking cups.

2. Whisk together the flour, baking powder, guar gum and salt in a large bowl. Make a well in the middle.

3. Add the grapeseed oil, applesauce, coconut nectar, vanilla and stevia and stir to combine. Next add the sunflower seed butter and stir to combine. Fold in ¾ cup of the chocolate chips.

4. Spoon the batter into the prepared muffin tin, filling the cups to the top, and top each with the remaining ½ cup of chocolate chips.

5. Bake the buttercups for 18 to 20 minutes, or until they are a light golden brown and bounce back slightly to the touch.

6. Transfer the muffin tin from the oven to a wire rack and let sit for about 15 minutes before removing the buttercups to cool completely.

Keep in an airtight container for up to 3 days, or wrap and freeze for up to 3 months.

Nutrition Information Per Serving (1 buttercup): 150 calories, 8 g total fat, 0.0 mg cholesterol, 18 g carbohydrates, 50 mg sodium, 2 g fiber, 3 g protein, 7 g sugars

CARAMEL GLAZED FAKIN' BACON BROWNIES

Makes 16 brownies

Like any nice Jewish girl from Queens, I grew up eating bacon for breakfast every now and then, on paper plates. This made it kosher. Nowadays, even though there is a plethora of fake bacon out there, it is highly processed and probably contains soy. Oy, what's an allergy mama to do? Well, I'll tell you in one word. Shitake. In addition to being a great source of vitamin C, iron and dietary fiber, shitake mushrooms, when baked, are a perfect impersonator of bacon. So enjoy these on a Sunday morning, and the house will smell just like cured meat. And you don't even have to use disposable tableware.

MUST HAVE

Faux Bacon

15 x 10-inch sheet of parchment paper

1 cup ¼-inch-thick sliced shitake mushrooms

1 tablespoon grapeseed oil

¼ teaspoon fine sea salt

Caramel Sauce

½ cup coconut nectar

¼ cup sunflower seed butter (see page 11)

¼ teaspoon fine sea salt

Brownies

Grapeseed oil, for greasing the pan

1¼ cups all-purpose gluten-free flour (see page 13)

½ cup cacao powder

½ teaspoon baking soda

⅜ teaspoon guar gum

¼ teaspoon fine sea salt

⅛ teaspoon cayenne powder (optional)

¼ cup grapeseed oil

¼ cup coconut nectar

1 teaspoon vanilla extract

⅜ teaspoon stevia powder

10 tablespoons warm water

MUST DO

1. Preheat oven to 350°F. Line a 15 x 10-inch jelly-roll pan with parchment paper.

2. To make the faux bacon, spread the shitake on the prepared pan. Drizzle the grapeseed oil on the mushrooms, toss them gently with your hands to coat and sprinkle with the salt. Bake for 40 minutes, or until the mushrooms are slightly crisp. Set aside.

3. Reduce the heat of the oven to 325°F.

4. To make the caramel sauce, mix together the coconut nectar, sunflower seed butter and salt in a small bowl until well combined.

5. To make the brownies, grease an 8 x 8-inch square baking pan with grapeseed oil.

6. Whisk together the flour, cacao powder, baking soda, guar gum, salt and cayenne, if using, in a large bowl.

7. Add the grapeseed oil, coconut nectar, vanilla and stevia and stir to combine. Next add the warm water and stir until it is absorbed and the batter is smooth.

8. Spoon the batter into the prepared pan, smooth down with a wet baking spatula or the back of a wet spoon and drizzle with caramel sauce. With a swirling motion, run a pointy knife in and out of the caramel sauce so some of it seeps into the brownie. Top evenly with the "bacon" bits.

9. Bake the brownies for 11 to 12 minutes, or until the batter starts to pull away from the sides of the pan and a toothpick inserted in the center comes out with just a few crumbs attached. Rotate the pan from front to back after 9 minutes of baking.

10. Transfer the pan from the oven to a wire rack and let rest for about 20 minutes before cutting the brownies into 16 squares.

Keep in an airtight container for up to 3 days, or wrap and freeze for up to 3 months.

Nutrition Information Per Serving (1 brownie):
120 calories, 6 g total fat, 0.0 mg cholesterol,
20 g carbohydrates, 140 mg sodium, 2 g fiber,
3 g protein, 8 g sugars

CHAPTER 5

A COOKIE IN THE HAND IS WORTH TWO IN LA BOUCHE

When I was a little girl, I wouldn't eat the cookie my mother put in my hand unless another one was firmly placed in the other. I can't tell you why I did this; it's not like I didn't know where my next snack was coming from. I guess it was a security issue. With a younger brother in tow, I never knew what might be left in the cookie jar. Now, my son, who's an only child, doesn't have to worry about siblings eating his rations—just his mother. Poor kid.

QUINOA CRANBERRY COOKIES

Makes about 12 cookies

One day I found my cupboards empty, save for quinoa flakes and dried cranberries. What kind of mother am I! So in need of some comfort, I used what I had and made my son some Quinoa Cranberry Cookies. Let me tell you, what a surprise it was to find that the blending of nutty-flavored quinoa flakes with sweet and tart dried cranberries was like a match made on JDate. Hey, don't knock online dating. That's how I met my husband. Anyway, even more than my tax return filing status, you should appreciate that when your kids eat these cookies, you can pat yourself on the back for getting them to eat their spinach. That's right. Quinoa is a complete, gluten-free protein grain that is related to the spinach family. And just so you know, these cookies are best right out of the oven, because they melt in your mouth like "butta."

MUST HAVE

15 x 13-inch sheet of parchment paper

1 cup quinoa flakes

¾ cup hot water

¾ cup all-purpose gluten-free flour (see page 13)

½ cup amaranth flour

½ teaspoon baking soda

¼ teaspoon cinnamon powder

¼ teaspoon ground nutmeg

¼ teaspoon guar gum

¼ teaspoon fine sea salt

¼ cup coconut oil

¼ cup coconut nectar

2 teaspoons vanilla extract

⅜ teaspoon stevia powder

¾ cup dried cranberries

MUST DO

1. Preheat oven to 325°F. Line a 15 x 13-inch cookie sheet with parchment paper.

2. Pour the quinoa flakes into a medium-size bowl, add the hot water and let sit without stirring.

3. Whisk together the two flours, baking soda, cinnamon, nutmeg, guar gum and salt in a large bowl. Make a well in the middle.

4. Microwave the coconut oil and coconut nectar in a 2-cup measuring cup for 20 seconds. Add the vanilla and stevia and stir to combine. Pour the coconut oil mixture into the flour mixture.

5. Next add the quinoa flake mixture and stir to combine. Fold in the dried cranberries.

6. Take about 1½ tablespoons of the dough, shape it into a ball, and place it on the prepared cookie sheet. Repeat until you have used up all the dough, placing the balls about 2 inches apart on the cookie sheet. Flatten each ball gently with the bottom of a measuring cup.

7. Bake the cookies for 16 to 18 minutes, or until they are a light golden brown around the edges. Rotate the cookie sheet from front to back after 10 minutes of baking.

8. Transfer the cookie sheet from the oven to a wire rack and let sit for about 10 minutes before removing the cookies to cool completely.

Keep in an airtight container for up to 3 days, or wrap and freeze for up to 3 months.

———◇———

Nutrition Information Per Serving (1 cookie): 145 calories, 5 g total fat, 0.0 mg cholesterol, 18 g carbohydrates, 80 mg sodium, 2 g fiber, 2 g protein, 10 g sugars

———◇———

Sweet Truth:

Use extra-virgin coconut oil if you want the final product to taste and smell like coconut. Otherwise, use refined coconut oil.

SUNFLOWER BUTTER CHOCOLATE CHIP COOKIES

Makes about 12 cookies

These cookies might freak you out, because they taste more like peanut butter cookies than peanut butter cookies. And better yet, as I hinted earlier, the selenium in sunflower seeds confer health benefits relating to men's virility, so that they are almost like Mother Nature's Viagra. So have your man keep some of these cookies socked away in his glove compartment, because you never know when the mood might strike.

MUST HAVE

15 x 13-inch sheet of parchment paper
1 cup all-purpose gluten-free flour (see page 13)
1 cup amaranth flour
½ teaspoon baking soda
½ teaspoon guar gum
½ teaspoon fine sea salt
¼ cup coconut nectar
3 tablespoons coconut oil
2 teaspoons vanilla extract
⅜ teaspoon stevia powder
½ cup sunflower seed butter (see page 11)
6 tablespoons water
¾ cup chocolate chips (see page 12)

MUST DO

1. Preheat oven to 325°F. Line a 15 x 13-inch cookie sheet with parchment paper.

2. Whisk together the two flours, baking soda, guar gum and salt in a large bowl. Make a well in the middle.

3. Microwave the coconut nectar and coconut oil in a 2-cup measuring cup for 20 seconds. Add the vanilla and stevia and stir to combine. Pour into the flour mixture.

4. Add the sunflower seed butter and water to the flour mixture and mix well. Fold in the chocolate chips.

5. Take about 1½ tablespoons of the dough, shape it into a ball, and place it on the prepared cookie sheet. Repeat until you have used up all the dough, placing the balls about 2 inches apart on the cookie sheet. Flatten each ball gently with the bottom of a measuring cup.

6. Bake the cookies for 18 to 20 minutes, or until they are a light golden brown around the edges. Rotate the cookie sheet from front to back halfway through baking.

7. Transfer the cookie sheet from the oven to a wire rack and let sit for about 10 minutes before removing the cookies to cool completely.

Keep in an airtight container for up to 3 days, or wrap individually and freeze for up to 3 months.

Nutrition Information Per Serving (1 cookie):
215 calories, 11 g total fat, 0.0 mg cholesterol,
29 g carbohydrates, 100 mg sodium, 2 g fiber,
3 g protein, 7 g sugars

OATMEAL FUDGE CHOCOLATE CHIP COOKIES

Makes about 12 cookies

Even though you may not think of putting chocolate in your child's bowl of oatmeal, there's no harm in doing so, as the antioxidant and mineral content of cacao powder is so immense, it's a natural juxtaposition to the high-fiber oats. But even better than that, the combinations of flavors can't be beat. So instead of hot cereal, I sometimes serve these cookies to my child as the first meal of the day, and I haven't heard a complaint yet.

MUST HAVE

15 x 13-inch sheet of parchment paper
1 cup all-purpose gluten-free flour (see page 13)
½ cup cacao powder
½ teaspoon baking soda
½ teaspoon guar gum
¼ teaspoon fine sea salt
¼ cup coconut oil
¼ cup coconut nectar
2 teaspoons vanilla extract
⅜ teaspoon stevia powder
½ cup water
1¼ cups gluten-free oats
¾ cup chocolate chips (see page 12)

MUST DO

1. Preheat oven to 325°F. Line a 15 x 13-inch cookie sheet with parchment paper.

2. Whisk together the flour, cacao powder, baking soda, guar gum and salt in a large bowl. Make a well in the middle.

3. Microwave the coconut oil and coconut nectar in a 2-cup measuring cup for 20 seconds. Add the vanilla and stevia and stir to combine. Pour into the flour mixture.

4. Add the water to the flour mixture and stir until the liquid is absorbed. Stir in the oats and chocolate chips.

5. Take about 1½ tablespoons of the dough, shape it into a ball, and place it on the prepared cookie sheet. Repeat until you have used up all the dough, placing the balls about 2 inches apart on the cookie sheet. Flatten each ball gently with the bottom of a measuring cup.

6. Bake the cookies for 12 to 13 minutes, or until the oats look a little dry and the kitchen smells like chocolate. Rotate the cookie sheet from front to back after 9 minutes of baking.

7. Transfer the cookie sheet from the oven to a wire rack and let sit for about 10 minutes before removing the cookies to cool completely.

Keep in an airtight container for up to 3 days, or wrap and freeze for up to 3 months.

Nutrition Information Per Serving (1 cookie): 160 calories, 7 g total fat, 0.0 mg cholesterol, 30 g carbohydrates, 100 mg sodium, 3 g fiber, 2 g protein, 6 g sugars

COSMIC CHOCOLATE CHIP COOKIES

Makes about 12 cookies

Face it, kids are the CEOs of their own microcosmic universe, and the adults who try to hack into this sacred space suck big-time. So the best thing to do to exist in the same stratum is to prepare yummies for their tummies that will make them think you're a superhero from Planet Kitchen. With the subtle spices ginger and nutmeg, overflowing with protective phytonutrients and exquisite flavor, I guarantee your kids will conclude that these Cosmic Chocolate Chip Cookies are out of this world!

MUST HAVE

15 x 13-inch sheet of parchment paper
1¼ cups all-purpose gluten-free flour (see page 13)
¾ cup amaranth flour
½ teaspoon baking soda
½ teaspoon guar gum
¼ teaspoon ginger powder
¼ teaspoon fine sea salt
⅛ teaspoon ground nutmeg
¼ cup coconut oil
¼ cup coconut nectar
1 tablespoon vanilla extract
¼ teaspoon orange extract
¼ teaspoon stevia powder
7 tablespoons water
¾ cup chocolate chips (see page 12)

MUST DO

1. Preheat oven to 325°F. Line a 15 x 13-inch cookie sheet with parchment paper.

2. Whisk together the two flours, baking soda, guar gum, ginger, salt and nutmeg in a large bowl. Make a well in the middle.

3. Microwave the coconut oil and coconut nectar in a 2-cup measuring cup for 20 seconds.

Add the vanilla, orange extract and stevia and stir to combine. Pour into the flour mixture.

4. Add the water to the flour mixture and stir until the liquid is absorbed. Fold in the chocolate chips.

5. Take about 1½ tablespoons of the dough, shape it into a ball, and place it on the prepared cookie sheet. Repeat until you have used up all the dough, placing the balls about 2 inches apart on the cookie sheet. Flatten each ball gently with the bottom of a measuring cup.

6. Bake the cookies for 12 to 13 minutes, or until they are a light golden brown around the edges. Rotate the cookie sheet from front to back after 9 minutes of baking.

7. Transfer the cookie sheet from the oven to a wire rack and let sit for about 10 minutes before removing the cookies to cool completely.

Keep in an airtight container for up to 3 days, or wrap and freeze for up to 3 months.

◇

Nutrition Information Per Serving (1 cookie): 170 calories, 7 g total fat, 0.0 mg cholesterol, 25 g carbohydrates, 100 mg sodium, 2 g fiber, 2 g protein, 7 g sugars

◇

PLUM LEMON PINKYPRINTS

Makes about 16 cookies

I think pinkies must be envious of their opposable neighbors four digits down. Let's face it. Thumbs get all the action. With thumb sucking, thumbs-ups, sticking out like a sore thumb, hitching a ride by way of thumb, being all thumbs if you're clumsy and holiday cookies called thumbprints, it's clear there is a prejudice. So I'm here to start the equal rights for pinkies movement by introducing my Plum Lemon Pinkyprints. They are now a hands-down favorite in my house.

MUST HAVE

Jam Filling

½ cup dried plums (aka prunes)

1 cup water

¼ cup freshly squeezed lemon juice

Cookies

15 x 13-inch sheet of parchment paper

1 cup all-purpose gluten-free flour (see page 13)

1 cup amaranth flour

½ teaspoon baking soda

½ teaspoon guar gum

¼ teaspoon fine sea salt

⅓ cup coconut oil

¼ cup coconut nectar

1 teaspoon vanilla extract

¼ teaspoon lemon extract

¼ teaspoon stevia powder

¼ cup water

MUST DO

1. To make the jam filling, boil the dried plums in the water in a medium-size saucepan for 15 minutes, or until very soft. Drain the water and place the plums and lemon juice in a food processor or blender and puree until smooth.

2. Preheat oven to 325°F. Line a 15 x 13-inch cookie sheet with parchment paper.

3. To make the cookies, whisk together the two flours, baking soda, guar gum and salt in a large bowl. Make a well in the middle.

4. Microwave the coconut oil and coconut nectar in a 2-cup measuring cup for 20 seconds. Add the vanilla, lemon extract and stevia and stir to combine. Pour into the flour mixture, add the water and stir until the liquid is absorbed.

5. Form the dough into marquise-shaped ovals, using about 1½ tablespoons for each, and place them about 2 inches apart on the prepared cookie sheet.

6. Gently press your pinkie, lengthwise, in the middle of each oval to form an indentation.

7. Spoon some plum lemon jam filling into each indentation. Dip your index finger into some water, and smooth out the top of the filling in each cookie with your wet finger.

8. Bake the pinkyprints for 17 to 18 minutes, or until they are a light golden brown. Rotate the cookie sheet from front to back after 10 minutes of baking.

9. Transfer the cookie sheet from the oven to a wire rack and let sit for about 10 minutes before removing the cookies to cool completely.

Keep in an airtight container for up to 3 days, or wrap and freeze for up to 3 months.

—————————◇—————————

Nutrition Information Per Serving (1 pinkyprint): 150 calories, 5 g total fat, 0.0 mg cholesterol, 24 g carbohydrates, 80 mg sodium, 2 g fiber, 2 g protein, 7 g sugars

—————————◇—————————

SICILIAN MANDEL BREAD

Makes about 12 cookies

Mandel bread is the Jewish answer to Italian biscotti. This is surprising, since Jews always answer a question with a question, not an answer. But in any event, I think Mandel is a little confused, because he's really a cookie, not a loaf. This crisp and herby cookie, twice baked, is good for dipping in and then sipping your beverage of choice.

MUST HAVE

15 x 13-inch sheet of parchment paper
1 cup all-purpose gluten-free flour (see page 13)
1 cup amaranth flour
5 tablespoons raw pumpkin seeds, coarsely chopped
1 teaspoon dried rosemary
1 teaspoon dried thyme
½ teaspoon baking soda
½ teaspoon guar gum
¼ teaspoon fine sea salt
¼ cup grapeseed oil
¼ cup coconut nectar
1 teaspoon vanilla extract
⅛ teaspoon stevia powder
½ cup water
1 teaspoon lemon zest

MUST DO

1. Preheat oven to 325°F. Line a 15 x 13-inch cookie sheet with parchment paper.

2. Whisk together the two flours, pumpkin seeds, rosemary, thyme, baking soda, guar gum and salt in a large bowl. Make a well in the middle.

3. Add the grapeseed oil, coconut nectar, vanilla and stevia and stir to combine. Next add the water and lemon zest and stir until incorporated.

4. Form the dough into a log and flatten it so that it is about 8 inches long and 4½ inches wide. Place the log on the prepared cookie sheet.

Sweet Truth:

When flattening the log before it's baked, it helps to put a piece of parchment paper and another cookie sheet on top of it and press down to ensure an even layer all the way across.

5. Bake the log for 25 to 26 minutes, or until it is a light golden brown and is firm to the touch. Rotate the cookie sheet from front to back halfway through baking.

6. Transfer the cookie sheet from the oven to a wire rack and let sit for about 10 minutes. Keep the oven on.

7. Place the log on a cutting board. Slice the log into ½-inch slices, on an angle, with a wet serrated knife. Arrange the slices on the cookie sheet, cut side down. Bake the

slices for 12 to 13 minutes, turning them
over halfway through baking, until both
sides are lightly toasted.

   8. Transfer the cookie sheet from the
oven to a wire rack and let sit for about 10
minutes before removing the cookies to
cool completely.

Keep in an airtight container for up to 3 days,
or wrap and freeze for up to 3 months.

————————◇————————

Nutrition Information Per Serving (1 cookie):
160 calories, 6 g total fat, 0.0 mg cholesterol,
24 g carbohydrates, 100 mg sodium, 2 g fiber,
3 g protein, 4 g sugars

————————◇————————

BASIL LEMONADE COOKIES

Makes about 12 cookies

The first thing I concocted when I bought my Vitamix blender was a Basil Lemonade Smoothie. I was growing basil in my backyard and had just planted a Meyer lemon tree in the front. I was excited to finally be able to "live off the land." The green lemonade was a big hit, so à la Hollywood, I made a sequel in a different format. Hopefully, it'll be a blockbuster in an oven near you.

MUST HAVE

Cookies

15 x 13-inch sheet of parchment paper

1½ cups all-purpose gluten-free flour (see page 13)

½ cup light buckwheat flour

½ teaspoon baking soda

½ teaspoon guar gum

¼ teaspoon fine sea salt

¼ cup coconut oil

¼ cup coconut nectar

1 teaspoon vanilla extract

½ teaspoon lemon extract

¼ teaspoon stevia powder

7 tablespoons water

3 tablespoons finely minced fresh basil

Lemon Glaze

1 tablespoon unsweetened coconut milk

¼ teaspoon turmeric powder

1 cup powdered erythritol

5 teaspoons freshly squeezed lemon juice

MUST DO

1. Preheat oven to 325°F. Line a 15 x 13-inch cookie sheet with parchment paper.

2. **To make the cookies**, whisk together the two flours, baking soda, guar gum and salt in a large bowl. Make a well in the middle.

3. Microwave the coconut oil and coconut nectar in a 2-cup measuring cup for 20 seconds. Add the vanilla, lemon extract and stevia and stir to combine. Pour into the flour mixture.

4. Add the water to the flour mixture and stir until the liquid is absorbed. Stir in the basil.

5. Take about 1½ tablespoons of the dough, shape it into a ball, and place it on the prepared cookie sheet. Repeat until you have used up all the dough, placing the balls about 2 inches apart on the cookie sheet. Flatten each gently with the bottom of a measuring cup.

6. Bake the cookies for 13 to 14 minutes, or until they are a light golden brown around the edges. Rotate the cookie sheet from front to back after 9 minutes of baking.

7. Transfer the cookie sheet from the oven to a wire rack and let sit for about 15 minutes before removing the cookies to cool completely.

8. **To make the lemon glaze**, mix together the coconut milk and turmeric powder in a medium-size microwave-safe bowl and microwave for 20 seconds. Add the powdered erythritol and lemon juice and stir until smooth and well combined.

9. Frost the completely cooled cookies.

Keep in an airtight container for up to 3 days, or wrap and freeze for up to 3 months.

Nutrition Information Per Serving (1 cookie): 125 calories, 5 g total fat, 0.0 mg cholesterol, 18 g carbohydrates, 100 mg sodium, 2 g fiber, 2 g protein, 4 g sugars

---

CHAPTER 6

CUPCAKE LOVE

One day a friend of mine told her four-year-old son that she loved him. He replied, "I love you, too, Mommy, but only when you give me cupcakes." So the demoralization of this tale is that at this age, a child's love is most likely cupcake conditional. Luckily, with these recipes, no matter what, a child can love these cupcakes and his or her mommy, too!

BLACK AND WHITE DELIGHT CUPCAKES

Makes 12 standard-size cupcakes

Since I'm from New York City, I was inspired to create these cupcakes as an ode to the classic delicatessen cookies of the same name. The cacao powder used for the "black" frosting in this recipe flows with flavonoids, compounds engaged in antioxidant activity, which helps reduce cellular damage caused by pesky free radicals. The "white" frosting contains erythritol, a natural, zero-calorie sweetener derived from fruits and vegetables. So in a world where most issues fall into the gray zone, it's comforting to know that you can count on your cupcakes to be black and white.

MUST HAVE

Cupcakes

12 standard-size paper baking cups

¾ cup unsweetened plain rice milk

1 teaspoon apple cider vinegar

1¾ cups all-purpose gluten-free flour (see page 13)

1 teaspoon sodium-free baking powder

½ teaspoon baking soda

⅜ teaspoon guar gum

¼ teaspoon fine sea salt

¼ cup grapeseed oil

¼ cup coconut nectar

2 teaspoons vanilla extract

¼ teaspoon lemon extract

⅜ teaspoon stevia powder

¼ cup vegan, soy-free plain yogurt
(I use So Delicious coconut milk yogurt. See resources for more information.)

Vanilla Frosting

1 cup powdered erythritol

2 tablespoons warm vanilla rice milk

1 tablespoon coconut oil

⅛ teaspoon fine sea salt

Chocolate Frosting

½ cup coconut nectar

3 tablespoons coconut oil

¾ cup cacao powder

2 tablespoons warm water

⅛ teaspoon stevia powder

⅛ teaspoon fine sea salt

MUST DO

1. Preheat oven to 325°F. Line a standard 12-cup cupcake tin with paper baking cups.

2. To make the cupcakes, mix together the rice milk and apple cider vinegar in a 2-cup measuring cup.

3. Whisk together the flour, baking powder, baking soda, guar gum and salt in a large bowl. Make a well in the middle.

4. Add the grapeseed oil, coconut nectar, vanilla, lemon extract and stevia to the flour

mixture and mix well to combine. Next add the rice milk mixture and stir until the liquid is absorbed and the batter is smooth. Stir in the yogurt until well combined.

5. Pour the batter into the measuring cup, as the spout will make it easier to pour the batter into the cupcake tin without spillage.

6. Pour the batter into the prepared cupcake tin, dividing it evenly. Each cup should be about two-thirds full. Bake the cupcakes for 15 to 16 minutes, or until they are a light golden brown and bounce back slightly to the touch. Rotate the cupcake tin from front to back after 10 minutes of baking.

7. Transfer the cupcake tin from the oven to a wire rack and let sit for 10 minutes before removing the cupcakes to cool completely.

8. **To make the vanilla frosting**, mix together the powdered erythritol and vanilla rice milk in a small bowl. Add the coconut oil and salt and stir until smooth and well combined.

9. **To make the chocolate frosting**, mix together the coconut nectar and coconut oil in a small bowl. Add the cacao powder, warm water, stevia and salt and stir until smooth and well combined.

10. Frost the completely cooled cupcakes, vanilla frosting on one half and chocolate frosting on the other.

Keep unfrosted cupcakes in an airtight container for up to 3 days, or wrap and freeze them for up to 3 months. Leftover frosting keeps in the fridge for about 4 weeks if stored in an airtight container.

Nutrition Information Per Serving (1 cupcake): 200 calories, 9 g total fat, 0.0 mg cholesterol, 23 g carbohydrates, 110 mg sodium, 2 g fiber, 2 g protein, 15 g sugars

CHOCOHOLIC CUPCAKES

Makes 12 standard-size cupcakes

No need for a twelve-step program here, because being addicted to chocolate, or these cupcakes, for that matter, is a good thing. Not only do you get the good stuff that chocolate brings, but I've also added a potassium boost thanks to the avocado in the frosting. The avocado adds not only health benefits but also a smooth creaminess, and no one but you will know it's in there.

MUST HAVE

Cupcakes

12 standard-size paper baking cups

1 cup unsweetened plain rice milk

1 teaspoon apple cider vinegar

1¾ cups all-purpose gluten-free flour (see page 13)

⅓ cup cacao powder

1¼ teaspoons sodium-free baking powder

1 teaspoon baking soda

½ teaspoon guar gum

¼ teaspoon fine sea salt

¼ cup grapeseed oil

¼ cup coconut nectar

2 teaspoons vanilla extract

⅜ teaspoon stevia powder

⅓ cup vegan, soy-free plain yogurt (I use So Delicious coconut milk yogurt. See resources for more information.)

Chocolate Frosting

1 cup coconut nectar

¼ cup coconut oil

¼ cup mashed avocado

2 cups powdered erythritol

1 cup cacao powder

2 tablespoons warm water

¼ teaspoon stevia powder

¼ teaspoon fine sea salt

MUST DO

1. Preheat oven to 325°F. Line a standard 12-cup cupcake tin with paper baking cups.

2. To make the cupcakes, mix together the rice milk and apple cider vinegar in a 2-cup measuring cup.

3. Whisk together the flour, cacao powder, baking powder, baking soda, guar gum and salt in a large bowl. Make a well in the middle.

4. Add the grapeseed oil, coconut nectar, vanilla and stevia to the flour mixture and stir to combine. Next add the rice milk mixture and stir until the liquid is absorbed and the batter is smooth. Stir in the yogurt until well combined.

5. Pour the batter into the measuring cup, as the spout will make it easier to pour the batter into the cupcake tin without spillage.

6. Pour the batter into the prepared cupcake tin, dividing it evenly. Each cup should be about two-thirds full. Bake the cupcakes for 16 to 17 minutes, or until they bounce back slightly to the touch. Rotate the cupcake tin from front to back after 10 minutes of baking.

7. Transfer the cupcake tin from the oven to a wire rack and let sit for 10 minutes before removing the cupcakes to cool completely.

8. To make the chocolate frosting, mix together the coconut nectar, coconut oil and mashed avocado in a large bowl. Add the powdered erythritol, cacao powder, warm water, stevia and salt and stir until smooth and well combined.

9. Frost the completely cooled cupcakes.

Keep unfrosted cupcakes in an airtight container for up to 3 days, or wrap and freeze them for up to 3 months. Leftover frosting keeps in the fridge for about 4 weeks if stored in an airtight container.

Nutrition Information Per Serving (1 cupcake): 180 calories, 9 g total fat, 0.0 mg cholesterol, 22 g carbohydrates, 135 mg sodium, 2 g fiber, 2 g protein, 12 g sugars

IRRESISTIBLE RED VELVET CUPCAKES

Makes 12 standard-size cupcakes

Most people go gaga over red velvet cake, but then some ask, "What's so great about it?" Since I'm Jewish, I answer a question with a question and ask back, "Well, what's so great about a diamond? Isn't it just a rock?" And that, girlfriend, is all that needs to be said, because that's really what red velvet cupcakes are. Edible diamonds. No?

MUST HAVE

Cupcakes

12 standard-size paper baking cups

10 ounces of frozen (thawed) cranberries

¼ cup water

2 tablespoons unsweetened plain rice milk

1 teaspoon apple cider vinegar

2 cups all-purpose gluten-free flour (see page 13)

1 tablespoon cacao powder

1½ teaspoons sodium-free baking powder

¼ teaspoon xanthan gum

¼ teaspoon fine sea salt

¼ cup grapeseed oil

¼ cup coconut nectar

1 teaspoon vanilla extract

⅜ teaspoon stevia powder

¼ cup fresh squeezed lemon juice

¼ teaspoon baking soda

Cranberry Frosting

2 tablespoons coconut oil

2 tablespoons coconut nectar

2½ cups powdered erythritol

¼ cup cranberry puree (leftover from cupcake preparation)

¼ teaspoon stevia powder

¼ teaspoon fine sea salt

MUST DO

1. Preheat oven to 325°F. Line a standard 12-cup cupcake tin with paper baking cups.

2. To make the cupcakes, place the cranberries and water in a food processor or blender and puree until smooth.

3. Mix together the rice milk and apple cider vinegar in a small bowl.

4. Whisk together the flour, cacao powder, baking powder, xanthan gum and salt in a large bowl. Make a well in the middle.

5. Add the grapeseed oil, coconut nectar, vanilla and stevia to the flour mixture and stir to combine. Next add the rice milk mixture and 1 cup of the cranberry puree, and stir until the liquid is absorbed and the batter is smooth.

6. Mix together the lemon juice and baking soda in a small bowl, wait till it fizzes, and then quickly stir it into the batter. Act swiftly here so the baking soda doesn't lose its potency once it hits the citric acid.

7. Spoon the batter into the prepared cupcake tin, dividing it evenly. Each cup should be about two-thirds full. Bake the cupcakes for 22 to 23 minutes, or until they bounce back slightly to the touch. Rotate the cupcake tin from front to back halfway through baking.

8. Transfer the cupcake tin from the oven to a wire rack and let sit for 30 minutes before removing the cupcakes to cool completely.

9. **To make the cranberry frosting,** microwave the coconut oil and coconut nectar in a medium-size microwave-safe bowl for 20 seconds. Add the powdered erythritol, the remaining ¼ cup of cranberry puree, stevia and salt and stir until smooth and well combined.

10. Frost the completely cooled cupcakes.

Keep unfrosted cupcakes in an airtight container for no longer than 1 day, or wrap and freeze them for up to 3 months. Leftover frosting keeps in the fridge for about 4 weeks if stored in an airtight container.

Nutrition Information Per Serving (1 cupcake): 175 calories, 7 g total fat, 0.0 mg cholesterol, 25 g carbohydrates, 110 mg sodium, 3 g fiber, 2 g protein, 7 g sugars

---

Sweet Truth:

I use xanthan gum instead of guar gum in this recipe because all the citric acid from the lemon juice renders guar gum ineffective. Speaking of lemon juice, only freshly squeezed works. If you use lemon juice from a bottle, the cupcakes will not retain their rosy color from the cranberries.

Sweet Truth:

Make sure to wait the entire time suggested before removing the baked cupcakes from their tin. Otherwise, you will have gummy cupcakes on your hands and you won't be very happy with me.

CRAZY FOR COCONUT CUPCAKES

Makes 12 standard-size cupcakes

The reason I'm so crazy for coconut, in all its various incarnations, is that scientific studies have shown it to have beneficial effects on the skin, hair, heart, liver, kidneys and bones, to boost immunity, and to aid digestion and weight management. "Weight management?" I can hear that incredulous tone in your voice. "Look at all those calories! Check out all those fat grams!" Well, it's true. Because it's a medium-chain fatty acid, coconut is more readily absorbed in your body, which causes it to increase your metabolism, which helps you burn more energy. So forget about that chichi weight loss program and eat these cupcakes for Jenny Craig's sake.

MUST HAVE

Cupcakes

12 standard-size paper baking cups

¾ cup unsweetened coconut milk

1 teaspoon apple cider vinegar

2 cups all-purpose gluten-free flour (see page 13)

⅓ cup unsweetened shredded coconut

1½ teaspoons sodium-free baking powder

¾ teaspoon baking soda

½ teaspoon guar gum

¼ teaspoon fine sea salt

¼ cup grapeseed oil

¼ cup coconut nectar

1 teaspoon vanilla extract

⅜ teaspoon stevia powder

⅓ cup vegan, soy-free plain yogurt
(I use So Delicious coconut milk yogurt.
See resources for more information.)

Coconut Butter Frosting

2 tablespoons coconut oil

2 tablespoons coconut nectar

2 cups powdered erythritol

½ cup sunflower seed butter (see page 11)

¼ cup unsweetened coconut milk

¼ teaspoon fine sea salt

Topping

½ cup unsweetened shredded coconut

MUST DO

1. Preheat oven to 325°F. Line a standard 12-cup cupcake tin with paper baking cups.

2. **To make the cupcakes**, mix together the coconut milk and apple cider vinegar in a 2-cup measuring cup.

3. Whisk together the flour, shredded coconut, baking powder, baking soda, guar gum and salt in a large bowl. Make a well in the middle.

4. Add the grapeseed oil, coconut nectar, vanilla and stevia to the flour mixture and stir to combine. Next add the coconut milk mixture and stir until it is absorbed. Stir in the yogurt until well combined.

5. Pour the batter into the measuring cup, as the spout will make it easier to pour the batter into the cupcake tin without spillage.

6. Pour the batter into the prepared cupcake tin, dividing it evenly. Each cup should be about two-thirds full. Bake the cupcakes for 15 to 16 minutes, or until they are a light golden brown and bounce back slightly to the touch. Rotate the cupcake tin from front to back after 10 minutes of baking.

7. Transfer the cupcake tin from the oven to a wire rack and let sit for 10 minutes before removing the cupcakes to cool completely.

8. **To make the coconut butter frosting**, microwave the coconut oil and coconut nectar in a medium-size microwave-safe bowl for 20 seconds. Add the powdered erythritol, sunflower seed butter, coconut milk and salt and stir until smooth and well combined.

9. Frost the completely cooled cupcakes.

10. Pour the shredded coconut into a small bowl. Roll the top of each frosted cupcake in the coconut topping to coat.

Keep unfrosted cupcakes in an airtight container for up to 3 days, or wrap and freeze them for up to 3 months. Leftover frosting keeps in the fridge for about 4 weeks if stored in an airtight container.

*Nutrition Information Per Serving (1 cupcake):
200 calories, 12 g total fat, 0.0 mg cholesterol,
25 g carbohydrates, 140 mg sodium, 3 g fiber,
3 g protein, 7 g sugars*

VIVID VANILLA CUPCAKES

Makes 12 standard-size cupcakes

This vanilla cupcake has a supermoist crumb and real vanilla bean speckled inside and out. A favorite among foodie toddlers.

MUST HAVE

Cupcakes

12 standard-size paper baking cups

¾ cup unsweetened plain rice milk

1 teaspoon apple cider vinegar

2 cups all-purpose gluten-free flour (see page 13)

1¼ teaspoons sodium-free baking powder

½ teaspoon baking soda

½ teaspoon guar gum

¼ teaspoon fine sea salt

¼ cup grapeseed oil

¼ cup coconut nectar

1 tablespoon vanilla extract

⅜ teaspoon stevia powder

⅓ cup vegan, soy-free plain yogurt
(I use So Delicious coconut milk yogurt.
See resources for more information.)

½ vanilla bean, cut in half lengthwise and
seeds scooped out and reserved

Vanilla Frosting

2½ cups powdered erythritol

6 tablespoons warm vanilla rice milk

2 tablespoons coconut oil

¼ teaspoon fine sea salt

½ vanilla bean, cut in half lengthwise and
seeds scooped out and reserved

MUST DO

1. Preheat oven to 325°F. Line a standard 12-cup cupcake tin with paper baking cups.

2. **To make the cupcakes,** mix together the rice milk and apple cider vinegar in a 2-cup measuring cup.

3. Whisk together the flour, baking powder, baking soda, guar gum and salt in a large bowl. Make a well in the middle.

4. Add the grapeseed oil, coconut nectar, vanilla and stevia to the flour mixture and stir to combine. Next add the rice milk mixture and stir until it is absorbed and the batter is smooth. Stir in the yogurt and vanilla bean seeds until well combined.

5. Pour the batter into the measuring cup, as the spout will make it easier to pour the batter into the cupcake tin without spillage.

6. Pour the batter into the prepared cupcake tin, dividing it evenly. Each cup should be about two-thirds full. Bake the cupcakes for 15 to 16 minutes, or until they are a light golden brown and bounce back slightly to the touch. Rotate the cupcake tin from front to back halfway through baking.

7. Transfer the cupcake tin from the oven to a wire rack and let sit for 10 minutes before removing the cupcakes to cool completely.

8. **To make the vanilla frosting**, mix together the powdered erythritol and warm vanilla rice milk in a medium-size bowl. Add the coconut oil and salt and stir until smooth and well incorporated. Stir in the vanilla bean seeds.

9. Frost the completely cooled cupcakes.

Keep unfrosted cupcakes in an airtight container for up to 3 days, or wrap and freeze them for up to 3 months. Leftover frosting keeps in the fridge for about 4 weeks if stored in an airtight container.

Nutrition Information Per Serving (1 cupcake):
190 calories, 9 g total fat, 0.0 mg cholesterol,
22 g carbohydrates, 130 mg sodium, 2 g fiber,
2 g protein, 6 g sugars

MOCHA ITALIAN ESPRESSO CUPCAKES

Makes 12 standard-size cupcakes

When I was a new mom, my favorite food group was caffeine. Since Peet's didn't accommodate my request for an IV of their Mocha Java Blend directly into my bloodstream, I was left to my own devices. This cupcake was the result. The tender and moist mocha cake gets an extra spike from an espresso frosting, which tops it off better than a thick spritz of foam on a venti Caffé Macchiato. . . . Or is that one of those "other" Seattle brands?

MUST HAVE

Cupcakes

12 standard-size paper baking cups

¾ cup unsweetened plain rice milk

¼ cup black coffee (room temperature)

1 teaspoon apple cider vinegar

2 cups all-purpose gluten-free flour (see page 13)

2 tablespoons espresso powder

1 tablespoon cacao powder

1¼ teaspoons sodium-free baking powder

1 teaspoon baking soda

½ teaspoon guar gum

¼ teaspoon fine sea salt

¼ cup grapeseed oil

¼ cup coconut nectar

2 teaspoons vanilla extract

⅜ teaspoon stevia powder

*⅓ cup vegan, soy-free plain yogurt
(I use So Delicious coconut milk yogurt.
See resources for more information.)*

Espresso Frosting

2 tablespoons coconut oil

2 tablespoons coconut nectar

2 cups powdered erythritol

2 tablespoons hot water

2 tablespoons espresso powder

¼ teaspoon fine sea salt

MUST DO

1. Preheat oven to 325°F. Line a standard 12-cup cupcake tin with paper baking cups.

2. **To make the cupcakes**, mix together the rice milk, coffee and apple cider vinegar in a 2-cup measuring cup.

3. Whisk together the flour, espresso powder, cacao powder, baking powder,

baking soda, guar gum and salt in a large bowl. Make a well in the middle.

4. Add the grapeseed oil, coconut nectar, vanilla and stevia to the flour mixture and stir to combine. Next add the rice milk–coffee mixture and stir until it is absorbed and the batter is smooth. Stir in the yogurt until well combined.

5. Pour the batter into the measuring cup, as the spout will make it easier to pour the batter into the cupcake tin without spillage.

6. Pour the batter into the prepared cupcake tin, dividing it evenly. Each cup should be about two-thirds full. Bake the cupcakes for 16 to 17 minutes, or until they bounce back slightly to the touch. Rotate the cupcake tin from front to back after 10 minutes of baking.

7. Transfer the cupcake tin from the oven to a wire rack and let sit for 10 minutes before removing the cupcakes to cool completely.

8. **To make the espresso frosting**, mix together the coconut oil and coconut nectar in a medium-size bowl. Add the powdered erythritol, hot water, espresso powder and salt and stir until smooth and well combined.

9. Frost the completely cooled cupcakes.

Keep unfrosted cupcakes in an airtight container for up to 3 days, or wrap and freeze them for up to 3 months. Leftover frosting keeps in the fridge for about 4 weeks if stored in an airtight container.

---

*Nutrition Information Per Serving (1 cupcake):
180 calories, 8 g total fat, 0.0 mg cholesterol,
23 g carbohydrates, 150 mg sodium, 2 g fiber,
2 g protein, 7 g sugars*

RUBY RED WINE AND CHOCOLATE CUPCAKES

Makes 12 standard-size cupcakes

I used to whine a lot during the week, until Friday came, but now I just add wine to my chocolate cupcakes and Friday comes rather quickly. You should try it; it's like having your very own cupcake vineyard right in your kitchen.

MUST HAVE

Cupcakes

12 standard-size paper baking cups

¾ cup unsweetened plain rice milk

¼ cup Pinot noir

1 teaspoon apple cider vinegar

1¾ cups all-purpose gluten-free flour (see page 13)

⅓ cup cacao powder

1¼ teaspoons sodium-free baking powder

1 teaspoon baking soda

½ teaspoon guar gum

¼ teaspoon fine sea salt

¼ cup grapeseed oil

¼ cup coconut nectar

2 teaspoons vanilla extract

⅜ teaspoon stevia powder

⅓ cup vegan, soy-free plain yogurt
(I use So Delicious coconut milk yogurt. See resources for more information.)

Chocolate Frosting

½ cup coconut nectar

2 tablespoons coconut oil

2 tablespoons mashed avocado

1 cup powdered erythritol

½ cup cacao powder

1 tablespoon warm water

⅛ teaspoon stevia powder

⅛ teaspoon fine sea salt

Pinot Noir Pink Frosting

½ tablespoon coconut oil

½ tablespoon coconut nectar

¾ cup powdered erythritol

½ tablespoon Pinot noir

½ tablespoon cranberry puree

⅛ teaspoon fine sea salt

MUST DO

1. Preheat oven to 325°F. Line a standard 12-cup cupcake tin with paper baking cups.

2. **To make the cupcakes**, mix together the rice milk, Pinot Noir and apple cider vinegar in a 2-cup measuring cup.

3. Whisk together the flour, cacao powder, baking powder, baking soda, guar gum and salt in a large bowl. Make a well in the middle.

4. Add the grapeseed oil, coconut nectar, vanilla and stevia to the flour mixture and stir to combine. Next add the rice milk mixture and stir until it is absorbed and the batter is smooth. Stir in the yogurt until well combined.

5. Pour the batter into the measuring cup, as the spout will make it easier to pour the batter into the cupcake tin without spillage.

6. Pour the batter into the prepared cupcake tin, dividing it evenly. Each cup should be about two-thirds full. Bake the cupcakes for 16 to 17 minutes, or until they bounce back slightly to the touch. Rotate the cupcake tin from front to back halfway through baking.

7. Transfer the cupcake tin from the oven to a wire rack and let sit for 10 minutes before removing the cupcakes to cool completely.

8. **To make the chocolate frosting**, mix together the coconut nectar, coconut oil and avocado in a medium-size bowl. Add the powdered erythritol, cacao powder, warm water, stevia and salt and stir until smooth and well incorporated.

9. **To make the Pinot noir pink frosting**, microwave the coconut oil and coconut nectar in a small microwave-safe bowl for 20 seconds. Add the powdered erythritol, Pinot noir, cranberry puree and salt and stir until smooth and well combined.

10. Frost the completely cooled cupcakes with the chocolate frosting. Place a dollop of the Pinot noir pink frosting on top.

Keep unfrosted cupcakes in an airtight container for up to 3 days, or wrap and freeze them for up to 3 months. Leftover frosting keeps in the fridge for about 4 weeks if stored in an airtight container.

Nutrition Information Per Serving (1 cupcake): 190 calories, 9 g total fat, 0.0 mg cholesterol, 23 g carbohydrates, 135 mg sodium, 2 g fiber, 2 g protein, 15 g sugars

Sweet Truth:

If you don't have cranberries on hand you can also use raspberry puree or beet puree to "pinken-up" the frosting.

CHAPTER 7

RAISING
THE BAR

I often speak to groups of people who are dealing with the challenges of either food allergies, celiac disease, diabetes or the munchies, and I invariably hear that there aren't enough nut-free, sugar-free or otherwise "safe" high-protein and healthful energy bars on the market. This chapter is my solution, so that everyone can have quick, delicious and nutritious fuel whenever they need it.

ANTIOXIDANT BLAST BARS

Makes 25 bars

Goji berries and blueberries top the charts when it comes to antioxidant content. I have included them, along with pumpkin seeds for a blast of protein, in this exquisitely crunchy, colorful and nutritious berry bar. The reason I don't use whole goji berries is that even though they start out bright and rosy red before they go in the oven, they come out an unappealing muddy shade of brown. Thank goodness for goji berry powder, which just disappears into the crowd while still providing all the promised nutrients.

MUST HAVE

Sheet of parchment paper slightly larger than 15 x 10 inches

4 cups gluten-free oats

1¾ cups all-purpose gluten-free flour (see page 13)

1 cup goji berry powder

1 cup raw pumpkin seeds, roughly chopped

1½ teaspoons guar gum

¼ teaspoon fine sea salt

1 cup coconut oil

½ cup coconut nectar

⅜ teaspoon stevia powder

1 cup fresh or frozen (thawed) blueberries

MUST DO

1. Preheat oven to 300°F. Line a 15 x 10-inch jelly-roll pan with parchment paper, with a little extra over the sides.

2. Mix together the oats, flour, goji berry powder, pumpkin seeds, guar gum and salt in a large bowl.

3. Microwave the coconut oil and coconut nectar in a 2-cup measuring cup for 60 seconds. Add the stevia and stir to combine. Pour the coconut oil mixture into the oats mixture and mix well. Fold in the blueberries.

4. Spoon the batter into the prepared pan and smooth it into the corners and on top with a wet baking spatula to cover the pan evenly.

5. Bake for 25 to 30 minutes, or until the oats are a light golden brown and look dry. Rotate the pan from front to back halfway through baking.

6. Transfer the pan from the oven to a wire rack and let sit for about 15 minutes before putting in the freezer for at least 1 hour.

7. Transfer the parchment paper to a cutting board and cut into 25 bars.

Wrap each bar individually in parchment paper or bakery tissue paper, place in a sealable plastic bag and keep frozen until ready to pack or eat.

Nutrition Information Per Serving (1 bar):
170 calories, 10 g total fat, 0.0 mg cholesterol,
25 g carbohydrates, 40 mg sodium, 4 g fiber,
3 g protein, 4 g sugars

Sweet Truth:

Wait until the bars are completely chilled before cutting into them, or else they will fall apart.

CHOCOLATE CHIA POWER BARS

Makes 25 bars

Beyond being a low-maintenance pet, chia is great because it is high in omega-3s, calcium, fiber, magnesium, niacin and potassium. Chia is also known to enhance endurance when doing strenuous activity. Combining this biodynamic seed with phytonutrient-rich cacao powder is a powerful energy bar waiting to be eaten.

Sweet Truth:

People who are allergic to mustard and sesame seeds may also be allergic to chia seeds.

MUST HAVE

Sheet of parchment paper slightly larger than 15 x 10 inches

4 cups gluten-free oats

1½ cups all-purpose gluten-free flour (see page 13)

1 cup unsweetened coconut chips (also called flaked coconut)

¾ cup raw sunflower seeds

⅓ cup cacao powder

3 tablespoons chia seeds

1½ teaspoons guar gum

¼ teaspoon fine sea salt

1 cup coconut oil

½ cup coconut nectar

¼ teaspoon stevia powder

1 cup fresh or frozen (thawed) cranberries, chopped

MUST DO

1. Preheat oven to 300°F. Line a 15 x 10-inch jelly-roll pan with parchment paper, with a little extra over the sides.

2. Mix together the oats, flour, coconut chips, sunflower seeds, cacao powder, chia seeds, guar gum and salt in a large bowl.

3. Microwave the coconut oil and coconut nectar in a 2-cup measuring cup for 60 seconds. Add the stevia and stir to combine. Pour into the oats mixture and mix well. Fold in the cranberries.

4. Spoon the batter into the prepared pan and smooth it into the corners and on top with a wet baking spatula to cover the pan evenly.

5. Bake for 25 to 30 minutes, or until the kitchen smells like chocolate and toasted oats. Rotate the pan from front to back halfway through baking.

6. Transfer the pan from the oven to a wire rack and let sit for about 15 minutes before putting in the freezer for at least 1 hour.

7. Transfer the parchment paper to a cutting board and cut into 25 bars.

Wrap each bar individually in parchment paper or bakery tissue paper, place in a sealable plastic bag and keep frozen until ready to pack or eat.

Nutrition Information Per Serving (1 bar): 180 calories, 11 g total fat, 0.0 mg cholesterol, 25 g carbohydrates, 40 mg sodium, 4 g fiber, 3 g protein, 4 g sugars

Sweet Truth:

Sometimes I break up one of these bars, put it in a bowl, add some rice milk or coconut milk and eat it as cereal.

SWEET CRANBERRY HEMP BARS

Makes 16 bars

Just in case there is some confusion, hemp seed has nothing to do with marijuana. So sorry to be the messenger on that one. But the good news is, instead of making you all high and hungry, hemp fills you up, levels off your blood sugar and contains heart-healthy omega-3 and omega-6, as well as vitamins A, B, D and E. So now you can have the high of your life just knowing that you're harboring such nutritious kernels in your snack.

MUST HAVE

Sheet of parchment paper slightly larger than 8 x 8 inches

1¾ cups gluten-free oats

⅓ cup all-purpose gluten-free flour (see page 13)

⅓ cup hemp seeds

⅜ teaspoon guar gum

¼ teaspoon fine sea salt

6 tablespoons coconut oil

6 tablespoons coconut nectar

¼ cup dried cranberries

MUST DO

1. Preheat oven to 325°F. Line an 8 x 8-inch square baking pan with parchment paper, with a little extra over the sides.

2. Mix together the oats, flour, hemp seeds, guar gum and salt in a large bowl.

3. Microwave the coconut oil and coconut nectar in a 2-cup measuring cup for 20 seconds and stir to combine. Pour the coconut oil mixture into the oat mixture. Fold in the dried cranberries.

4. Spoon the batter into the prepared pan and smooth it into the corners and on top with a wet baking spatula to cover the pan evenly.

5. Bake for 24 to 25 minutes, or until the oats are a light golden brown. Rotate the pan from front to back halfway through baking.

6. Transfer the pan from the oven to a wire rack and let sit for about 15 minutes before putting in the freezer for at least 1 hour.

7. Transfer the parchment paper to a cutting board and cut into 16 bars.

Wrap each bar individually in parchment paper or bakery tissue paper, place in a sealable plastic bag and keep frozen until ready to pack or eat.

Nutrition Information Per Serving (1 bar): 100 calories, 6 g total fat, 0.0 mg cholesterol, 19 g carbohydrates, 40 mg sodium, 2 g fiber, 2 g protein, 5 g sugars

FUDGY FIG-A-MAMA-JIG BARS

Makes 25 bars

You should do a jig when your kids eat figs because they are high in calcium, iron and potassium. The only way I used to eat figs was by way of Fig Newtons. These remind me a little of those. They have a touch of fudge that won't add any pudge.

MUST HAVE

Sheet of parchment paper slightly larger than 15 x 10 inches

12 dried Calimyrna figs, de-stemmed and cut into ½-inch pieces

3 tablespoons water

4 cups gluten-free oats

1½ cups all-purpose gluten-free flour (see page 13)

¾ cup raw pumpkin seeds, roughly chopped

⅓ cup cacao powder

1 teaspoon guar gum

¼ teaspoon fine sea salt

1 cup coconut oil

½ cup coconut nectar

¼ teaspoon stevia powder

MUST DO

1. Preheat oven to 300°F. Line a 15 x 10-inch jelly-roll pan with the parchment paper, with a little extra over the sides.

2. Place the figs and water in a food processor or blender and puree.

3. Mix together the oats, flour, pumpkin seeds, cacao powder, guar gum and salt in a large bowl.

4. Microwave the coconut oil and coconut nectar in a 2-cup measuring cup for 60 seconds. Add the stevia and stir to combine. Pour the coconut oil mixture into the oats mixture. Fold in the fig puree.

5. Spoon the batter into the prepared pan and smooth it into the corners and on top with a wet baking spatula to cover the pan evenly.

6. Bake for 25 to 30 minutes, or until the oats are a dark golden brown and look dry. Rotate the pan halfway through baking.

7. Transfer the pan from the oven to a wire rack and let sit for about 15 minutes before putting in the freezer for at least 1 hour.

8. Transfer the parchment paper to a cutting board and cut into 25 bars.

Wrap each bar individually in parchment paper or bakery tissue paper, place in a sealable plastic bag and keep frozen until ready to pack or eat.

Nutrition Information Per Serving (1 bar): 150 calories, 8 g total fat, 0.0 mg cholesterol, 27 g carbohydrates, 40 mg sodium, 4 g fiber, 3 g protein, 6 g sugars

LEAN GREEN LOGS—UNBAKED

Makes about 14 logs

I went through a raw phase. The first time I served my husband raw lasagna, he almost walked out. So I stopped making his meals that way, but I saved an extra-special treat for myself. So now it's yours, too, and I give you permission not to share. Also, unlike my grandparents in Florida, spirulina does not like the heat, which is the reason these bars are unbaked. But as you'll see in the recipe, the groats are cooked, so Sandra Lee might say these bars are semi-raw. The toasted groats lend a Nestlé Crunch–like "snap, crack and pop" quality to these bars, which will give you bowls more fun than hearing your cereal talk.

MUST HAVE

Logs

15 x 10-inch sheet of parchment paper

1 cup water, plus 3 tablespoons for the date and fig puree

½ cup buckwheat groats

10 Medjool dates, pitted and halved

6 dried Calimyrna figs, de-stemmed and halved

⅓ cup hemp seeds

¼ cup goji berries

2 teaspoons cacao powder

¾ teaspoon spirulina powder

¼ teaspoon Matcha green tea powder

¼ teaspoon ginger powder

⅛ teaspoon fine sea salt

½ cup raw pumpkin seeds, roughly chopped

Chocolate Glaze

1 four-ounce bar 100 percent unsweetened chocolate, chopped

2 tablespoons coconut oil

2 tablespoons coconut nectar

⅛ teaspoon stevia powder

⅛ teaspoon fine sea salt

MUST DO

1. Preheat oven to 375°F. Line a 15 x 10-inch jelly-roll pan with parchment paper.

2. **To make the logs**, combine the 1 cup water and the buckwheat groats in a medium-size saucepan and bring to a boil. Reduce the heat and simmer for about 15 minutes, or until all the water is absorbed. Spread the groats out on the prepared pan and bake in the oven for 30 minutes, or until the groats are very crunchy. There should not be a soggy one in the bunch. Toss the groats halfway through baking.

3. Combine the dates, figs and the 3 tablespoons water in a food processor or blender and puree. Spoon the date-fig puree into a large bowl.

4. Add the hemp seeds, goji berries, cacao powder, spirulina powder, Matcha green tea powder, ginger and salt to the date-fig puree and stir to combine. Fold in the toasted buckwheat groats and pumpkin seeds.

5. Take about 1 tablespoon of the "dough," and with wet hands, shape it into a log. Place

the log on the prepared pan that was used to toast the groats. Repeat until you have used up all the dough. Place the logs in the freezer to chill while you make the chocolate glaze.

6. **To make the chocolate glaze**, combine the chocolate, coconut oil and coconut nectar in a small microwave-safe bowl and microwave for 30 seconds at a time until the chocolate melts. Add the stevia and salt and stir to combine.

7. Take the logs out of the freezer, dip each into the melted chocolate and set back down on the pan. Place the glazed logs back in the freezer to chill for 2 hours.

Wrap each log individually in parchment paper or bakery tissue paper, place in a

sealable plastic bag and keep frozen until ready to pack or eat.

Nutrition Information Per Serving (1 log):
135 calories, 6 g total fat, 0.0 mg cholesterol,
19 g carbohydrates, 40 mg sodium, 3 g fiber,
3 g protein, 8 g sugars

Sweet Truth:

The beauty of parchment paper is that it can be reused several times before you have to discard it, as seen in this recipe.

AÇAÍ BERRY TRUFFLES—UNBAKED

Makes about 18 truffles

If a blueberry walked into a bar and hooked up with a cosmopolitan piece of chocolate sass, you would get a taste of açaí. A popular berry from Brazil, açaí conveniently comes in powdered form, so you can easily add it to this energy bar. It is filled with calcium and vitamins A, B_6 and E and is high in antioxidants, but it loses its potency if heated.

MUST HAVE

Truffles

8 x 8-inch sheet of parchment paper

12 Medjool dates, pitted and halved

1 cup raw sunflower seeds

1 cup raw pumpkin seeds

3 tablespoons açaí powder

3 tablespoons frozen (thawed) cranberries

3 tablespoons freshly squeezed orange juice

2 teaspoons cacao powder

⅛ teaspoon fine sea salt

Topping

½ cup unsweetened shredded coconut

MUST DO

1. Line an 8 x 8-inch square baking pan with parchment paper.

2. Combine the dates, sunflower seeds, pumpkin seeds, açaí powder, cranberries, orange juice, cacao powder and salt in a food processor or blender and process until almost smooth.

3. Take about 1 tablespoon of the date mixture, and with wet hands, shape it into a ball. Place the ball on the prepared pan. Repeat until you have used up all the date mixture.

4. Pour the shredded coconut into a small bowl. Roll each ball in the coconut and place it back on the prepared pan. Put the truffles in the freezer to chill for at least 1 hour.

Place the truffles in a sealable plastic bag and keep them frozen until ready to eat.

Nutrition Information Per Serving (1 truffle): 110 calories, 5 g total fat, 0.0 mg cholesterol, 15 g carbohydrates, 30 mg sodium, 3 g fiber, 3 g protein, 9 g sugars

RIGHT: *Açaí Berry Truffles and Seedy Date Balls*

SEEDY DATE BALLS—UNBAKED

Makes about 14 seedy balls

No, this recipe has nothing to do with blind dates or terrible pickup lines. This was the best name for these balls. Seeds are a perfect source of quick energy and contain all the amino acids, omegas, vitamins, minerals, enzymes and fiber your body needs. With no heat hitting them, the live enzymes stay intact.

MUST HAVE

Date Balls

8 x 8-inch sheet of parchment paper

6 Medjool dates, pitted and halved

6 dried plums (aka prunes), pitted and cut into ½-inch pieces

½ cup raw sunflower seeds

½ cup raw pumpkin seeds

¼ cup chocolate chips (see page 12)

¼ cup fresh or frozen (thawed) blueberries

1 teaspoon cacao powder

¼ teaspoon fine sea salt

3 tablespoons water

Topping

¼ cup chia seeds

MUST DO

1. Line an 8 x 8-inch square baking pan with parchment paper.

2. Combine the dates, plums, sunflower seeds, pumpkin seeds, chocolate chips, blueberries, cacao powder, salt and water in a food processor or blender and process until almost smooth.

3. Take about 1 tablespoon of the date-plum mixture, and with wet hands, shape it into a ball. Place the ball on the prepared pan. Repeat until you have used up all the date-plum mixture.

4. Pour the chia seeds into a small bowl. Roll each ball in the chia seeds and place it back on the prepared pan. Place the balls in the freezer to chill for 2 hours.

Wrap each ball individually in parchment paper or bakery tissue paper, place in a sealable plastic bag and keep frozen until ready to pack or eat.

Nutrition Information Per Serving (1 ball): 80 calories, 3 g total fat, 0.0 mg cholesterol, 12 g carbohydrates, 20 mg sodium, 3 g fiber, 2 g protein, 7 g sugars

CHAPTER 8

BAKED DONUT HOLES

Some people may take a firm stand against healthy donut holes, insisting that donuts should not, in any way, shape or form, possess any nutritional value. But since you're reading this book, I know you beg to differ. So here are some scrumptious donut recipes just for you, in all their unhole-y wholesomeness.

APPLE FRITTER DONUT HOLES

Makes about 20 donut holes

Maybe it has something to do with Eve, but every gal I know just loves a sugar-stuffed, fat-filled apple fritter every now and then. It's obviously a sinfully delicious fete for your palate, but here I've made it healthful and festive by inviting cinnamon, sunflower seed butter and an apple cider–lemon glaze to the (dough) ball. I guarantee that your banishment from the Garden will be of no consequence due to the gratification you will receive from taking a bite from this sweet apple.

MUST HAVE

Donut Holes

15 x 10-inch sheet of parchment paper

1½ cups all-purpose gluten-free flour (see page 13)

¼ cup light buckwheat flour

½ teaspoon cinnamon powder

¼ teaspoon sodium-free baking powder

¼ teaspoon guar gum

¼ teaspoon fine sea salt

¼ cup unsweetened plain rice milk

3 tablespoons coconut nectar

2 tablespoons sunflower seed butter (see page 11)

1 tablespoon freshly squeezed lemon juice

1 teaspoon vanilla extract

¼ teaspoon stevia powder

⅓ cup grated, peeled Granny Smith apple

Apple Cider–Lemon Glaze

1 tablespoon coconut nectar

1 tablespoon coconut oil

1 cup powdered erythritol

2 tablespoons freshly squeezed lemon juice

1 tablespoon apple cider

Topping

¾ teaspoon cinnamon powder

MUST DO

1. Preheat oven to 325°F. Line a 15 x 10-inch jelly-roll pan with parchment paper.

2. To make the donut holes, whisk together the two flours, cinnamon, baking powder, guar gum and salt in a large bowl. Make a well in the middle.

3. Add the rice milk, coconut nectar, sunflower seed butter, lemon juice, vanilla and stevia to the flour mixture and stir to combine. Fold in the grated apple.

4. Take about ½ tablespoon of the dough and shape it into a ball. Place the ball on the prepared pan. Repeat until you have used up all the dough, placing the balls about 2 inches apart on the pan.

5. Bake the donut holes for 12 to 13 minutes, or until they are a light golden brown and bounce back slightly to the touch. Rotate the pan from front to back after about 9 minutes of baking.

6. Transfer the pan from the oven to a wire rack and let sit for 10 minutes before removing the donut holes to cool completely.

7. **To make the apple cider–lemon glaze**, microwave the coconut nectar and coconut oil in a 2-cup measuring cup for 20 seconds. Add the powdered erythritol, lemon juice and apple cider and stir to combine.

8. Frost each donut hole with the glaze, sprinkle a little cinnamon on each and place on the wire rack to set.

Keep in an airtight container for up to 3 days, or wrap and freeze for up to 3 months.

———————◇———————

Nutrition Information Per Serving (1 donut hole):
60 calories, 2 g total fat, 0.0 mg cholesterol,
12 g carbohydrates, 30 mg sodium, 1 g fiber,
2 g protein, 4 g sugars

———————◇———————

DOUBLE CHOCOLATE CHIP GLAZED-OVER DONUT HOLES

Makes about 20 donut holes

I usually judge how happy a person's home is by how much chocolate they have in it. I've always been a chocolate person, and I especially have always liked chocolate donuts. Ever since I was old enough to place an over-the-counter donut order, I've faithfully asked for the Chocolate Glazed, rudely ignoring the other, just as capable donuts. But after years of suffering the consequences of the donut's sugar, fat and who knows what else, I was compelled to create a healthier version. It's just as delicious as the original version, if not more so, and judging by the gallon bags filled with these donuts in my freezer, they keep my homeys and me very happy.

MUST HAVE

Donut Holes

15 x 10-inch sheet of parchment paper

1½ cups all-purpose gluten-free flour (see page 13)

2 tablespoons cacao powder

¼ teaspoon guar gum

¼ teaspoon fine sea salt

⅛ teaspoon baking soda

¼ cup coconut nectar

3 tablespoons coconut oil

¼ cup unsweetened plain rice milk

1 tablespoon plum lemon jam (see page 61)

1 teaspoon vanilla extract

½ teaspoon orange extract

¼ teaspoon stevia powder

⅓ cup chocolate chips (see page 12)

Glaze

1 tablespoon coconut oil

1 tablespoon coconut nectar

2 tablespoons cacao powder

1 tablespoon water

½ cup powdered erythritol

⅛ teaspoon fine sea salt

MUST DO

1. Preheat oven to 325°F. Line a 15 x 10-inch jelly-roll pan with parchment paper.

2. **To make the donut holes**, whisk together the flour, cacao powder, guar gum, salt and baking soda in a large bowl. Make a well in the middle.

3. Microwave the coconut nectar and coconut oil in a 2-cup measuring cup for 20 seconds. Add the rice milk, plum lemon jam, vanilla, orange extract and stevia. Pour into the flour mixture and stir to combine. Fold in the chocolate chips.

4. Take about ½ tablespoon of the dough and shape it into a ball. Place the ball on the prepared pan. Repeat until you have used up all the dough, placing the balls about 2 inches apart on the pan.

5. Bake the donut holes for 11 to 12 minutes, or until they spring back slightly to the touch. Rotate the pan from front to back after about 9 minutes of baking.

6. Transfer the pan from the oven to a wire rack and let sit for 10 minutes before removing the donut holes to cool completely.

7. **To make the glaze**, microwave the coconut oil and the coconut nectar in a measuring cup for 20 seconds. Add the cacao powder, water, powdered erythritol and salt and stir to combine.

8. Frost each donut hole with the glaze and place on the wire rack to set.

Keep in an airtight container for up to 3 days, or wrap and freeze for up to 3 months.

———◇———

Nutrition Information Per Serving (1 donut hole): 60 calories, 3 g total fat, 0.0 mg cholesterol, 12 g carbohydrates, 60 mg sodium, 1 g fiber, 1 g protein, 4 g sugars

———◇———

BLUEBERRY STREUSEL DONUT HOLES

Makes about 20 donut holes

Since streusel is a blueberry's BFF, it is always a natural topping choice. Blueberries can certainly make a go of it on their own in any dessert, as they burst with tangy sweetness and anthocyanin, the antioxidant responsible for them getting the pigment blues. But it's nice to know that when your blueberry is down a donut hole, some streusel has it covered.

MUST HAVE

Donut Holes

15 x 10-inch sheet of parchment paper

1½ cups all-purpose gluten-free flour (see page 13)

¼ cup gluten-free oats, ground
(use a coffee grinder or food processor)

½ teaspoon cinnamon powder

¼ teaspoon guar gum

¼ teaspoon sodium-free baking powder

¼ teaspoon fine sea salt

⅛ teaspoon baking soda

¼ cup coconut nectar

3 tablespoons coconut oil

¼ cup unsweetened plain rice milk

1 teaspoon lemon extract

¼ teaspoon stevia powder

½ cup fresh or frozen (thawed) blueberries

Streusel

½ cup gluten-free oats, ground
(use a coffee grinder or food processor)

½ teaspoon cinnamon powder

MUST DO

1. Preheat oven to 325°F. Line a 15 x 10-inch jelly-roll pan with parchment paper.

2. **To make the donut holes,** whisk together the flour, the ¼ cup of ground oats, cinnamon, guar gum, baking powder, salt and baking soda in a large bowl. Make a well in the middle.

3. Microwave the coconut nectar and coconut oil in a 2-cup measuring cup for 20 seconds. Add the rice milk, lemon extract and stevia and stir to combine. Pour into the flour mixture and stir until the liquid is absorbed. Fold in the blueberries.

4. Take about ½ tablespoon of the dough and shape it into a ball. Place the ball on the prepared pan. Repeat until you have used up all the dough.

5. **To make the streusel,** mix together the ½ cup of ground oats and the cinnamon in a small bowl.

6. Roll the dough balls in the streusel and place them about 2 inches apart on the prepared pan.

7. Bake the donut holes for 11 to 12 minutes, or until they are a light golden brown and bounce back slightly to the touch. Rotate the pan from front to back after about 9 minutes of baking.

8. Transfer the pan from the oven to a wire rack and let sit for 10 minutes before removing the donut holes to cool completely.

Keep in an airtight container for up to 3 days, or wrap and freeze for up to 3 months.

Nutrition Information Per Serving (1 donut hole):
50 calories, 1 g total fat, 0.0 mg cholesterol,
13 g carbohydrates, 50 mg sodium, 1 g fiber,
1 g protein, 4 g sugars

Sweet Truth:

The oats should be coarsely ground, not too fine, as this lends the donut holes and the streusel a nicer texture.

PUMPKIN SPICE DONUT HOLES

Makes about 20 donut holes

Every October I take my son to the makeshift neighborhood pumpkin patch, where, in addition to hundreds of pumpkins of various sizes, shapes and colors, there are wagon rides, toys, games, pony rides, candy and scary stuffed stuff. It's like a vortex I get sucked into and can't get out of for at least four hours. And they have not one porta-potty! Since it seems my bladder shrinks in direct proportion to the scarcity of a local toilet, I hastily leave the patch to find relief, and—more often than not—forget to buy a pumpkin. That's why I use canned organic pumpkin here. At least Whole Foods has restrooms.

MUST HAVE

Donut Holes

15 x 10-inch sheet of parchment paper

1½ cups all-purpose gluten-free flour (see page 13)

¼ cup light buckwheat flour

2 teaspoons pumpkin pie spice

¼ teaspoon sodium-free baking powder

¼ teaspoon guar gum

¼ teaspoon fine sea salt

¼ cup coconut nectar

1 tablespoon coconut oil

3 tablespoons unsweetened plain rice milk

¼ teaspoon stevia powder

5 tablespoons canned pumpkin puree

Cinnamon Dust

¼ cup cinnamon powder

MUST DO

1. Preheat oven to 325°F. Line a 15 x 10-inch jelly-roll pan with parchment paper.

2. Whisk together the two flours, pumpkin pie spice, baking powder, guar gum and salt in a large bowl. Make a well in the middle.

3. Microwave the coconut nectar and coconut oil in a 2-cup measuring cup for 20 seconds. Add the rice milk and stevia and stir to combine. Pour into the flour mixture. Add the pumpkin puree and stir to combine.

4. Take about ½ tablespoon of the dough and shape it into a ball. Place the ball on the prepared pan. Repeat until you have used up all the dough.

5. Pour the cinnamon into a small bowl. Roll the dough balls in the cinnamon and place them about 2 inches apart on the prepared pan.

6. Bake the donut holes for 11 to 12 minutes, or until they are golden orange and bounce back slightly to the touch. Rotate the pan from front to back halfway through baking.

7. Transfer the pan from the oven to a wire rack and let sit for 10 minutes before removing the donut holes to cool completely.

Keep in an airtight container for up to 3 days, or wrap and freeze for up to 3 months.

Nutrition Information Per Serving (1 donut hole):
50 calories, 2 g total fat, 0.0 mg cholesterol,
12 g carbohydrates, 40 mg sodium, 1 g fiber,
1 g protein, 4 g sugars

VANILLA BEAN–GLAZED BANANA DONUT HOLES

Makes about 20 donut holes

I once took so much banana bread at an all-you-can-eat restaurant that my date had to physically hold me down to keep me from going back for more. That's when I decided to move three thousand miles away and develop my own banana bread recipes so I wouldn't be seen in public ever again putting banana bread in my pocketbook. So here's a donut hole that reminds me of that era, but this time no one is holding me back from loading up my clutch.

MUST HAVE

Donut Holes

15 x 10-inch sheet of parchment paper

1½ cups all-purpose gluten-free flour (see page 13)

2 tablespoons amaranth flour

¼ teaspoon sodium-free baking powder

¼ teaspoon ground nutmeg

¼ teaspoon guar gum

¼ teaspoon fine sea salt

3 tablespoons coconut nectar

2 tablespoons coconut oil

2 tablespoons vanilla rice milk

1 teaspoon vanilla extract

¼ teaspoon stevia powder

¼ cup mashed banana

Vanilla Bean Glaze

1 tablespoon coconut oil

1 tablespoon coconut nectar

1 cup powdered erythritol

2 tablespoons vanilla rice milk

⅛ teaspoon fine sea salt

¼ vanilla bean, cut in half lengthwise and seeds scooped out and reserved

MUST DO

1. Preheat oven to 325°F. Line a 15 x 10-inch jelly-roll pan with parchment paper.

2. To make the donut holes, whisk together the two flours, baking powder, nutmeg, guar gum and salt in a large bowl. Make a well in the middle.

3. Microwave the coconut nectar and coconut oil in a 2-cup measuring cup for 20 seconds. Add the rice milk, vanilla and stevia and stir to combine. Pour into the flour mixture, add the mashed banana and stir to combine.

4. Take about ½ tablespoon of the dough and shape it into a ball. Place the ball on the prepared pan. Repeat until you have used up all the dough, placing the balls about 2 inches apart on the prepared pan.

5. Bake the donut holes for 11 to 12 minutes, or until they are a light golden brown and bounce back slightly to the touch. Rotate the pan from front to back after about 9 minutes of baking.

6. Transfer the pan from the oven to a wire rack and let sit for 10 minutes before removing the donut holes to cool completely.

7. To make the vanilla bean glaze, microwave the coconut oil and coconut nectar in a measuring cup for 20 seconds. Add the powdered erythritol, vanilla rice milk and salt and stir to combine. Next add the vanilla bean seeds and mix well.

8. Frost the donut holes with the glaze and place them on the wire rack to set.

Keep in an airtight container for up to 3 days, or wrap and freeze for up to 3 months.

Nutrition Information Per Serving (1 donut hole): 60 calories, 3 g total fat, 0.0 mg cholesterol, 12 g carbohydrates, 30 mg sodium, 1 g fiber, 1 g protein, 4 g sugars

COCONUT CRUNCH DONUT HOLES

Makes about 20 donut holes

There is a misconception out there that the coconut is a tree nut because it ends with the letters "n-u-t" and grows on a "t-r-e-e." But I assure you the coconut is a drupe, which means it's a fibrous, one-seeded piece of fruit. So next time someone mistakenly declares that coconuts are tree nuts, you should ask them if donuts are "n-u-t-s," as well.

MUST HAVE

Donut Holes

15 x 10-inch sheet of parchment paper

1¼ cups all-purpose gluten-free flour (see page 13)

¼ cup amaranth flour

2 tablespoons unsweetened shredded coconut

¼ teaspoon sodium-free baking powder

¼ teaspoon guar gum

¼ teaspoon fine sea salt

¼ cup coconut nectar

2 tablespoons coconut oil

¼ cup unsweetened coconut milk

1 teaspoon vanilla extract

¼ teaspoon stevia powder

Topping

1 cup unsweetened shredded coconut

¼ cup unsweetened coconut milk

MUST DO

1. Preheat oven to 325°F. Line a 15 x 10-inch jelly-roll pan with parchment paper.

2. Whisk together the two flours, shredded coconut, baking powder, guar gum and salt in a large bowl. Make a well in the middle.

3. Microwave the coconut nectar and coconut oil in a 2-cup measuring cup for 20 seconds. Add the coconut milk, vanilla and stevia and stir to combine. Pour into the flour mixture and stir until the liquid is absorbed.

4. Take about ½ tablespoon of the dough and shape it into a ball. Place the ball on the prepared pan. Repeat until you have used up all the dough.

5. Pour the shredded coconut into a small bowl and the coconut milk into a cup. Dip the dough balls, one by one, in the coconut milk, roll them around in the shredded coconut and place them about 2 inches apart on the prepared pan.

6. Bake the donut holes for 12 to 13 minutes, or until they bounce back slightly to the touch. Rotate the pan from front to back after about 9 minutes of baking.

7. Transfer the pan from the oven to a wire rack and let sit for 10 minutes before removing the donut holes to cool completely.

Keep in an airtight container for up to 3 days, or wrap individually and freeze for up to 3 months.

Nutrition Information Per Serving (1 donut hole): 70 calories, 3 g total fat, 0.0 mg cholesterol, 12 g carbohydrates, 30 mg sodium, 1 g fiber, 1 g protein, 3 g sugars

SAFFRON AND CARDAMOM DONUT HOLES

Makes about 20 donut holes

I have a great affinity to saffron. Its exquisite aroma, taste and health benefits far outweigh the fact that it is a tad expensive. But let me be the first to tell you, you're worth it! The combination of this antiaging, vitamin- and mineral-containing über-herb is like a pea in the cardamom pod. The complementary elements of spice and sophistication make this a donut hole in one.

MUST HAVE

Donut Holes

15 x 10-inch sheet of parchment paper

¼ cup unsweetened plain rice milk

⅛ teaspoon crushed saffron threads

¼ cup coconut nectar

2 tablespoons coconut oil

½ teaspoon lemon extract

¼ teaspoon stevia powder

1¾ cups all-purpose gluten-free flour (see page 13)

¼ teaspoon sodium-free baking powder

¼ teaspoon ground cardamom

¼ teaspoon guar gum

¼ teaspoon fine sea salt

Saffron Glaze

2 tablespoons unsweetened plain rice milk

1 tablespoon coconut nectar

⅛ teaspoon crushed saffron threads

1 cup powdered erythritol

⅛ teaspoon fine sea salt

MUST DO

1. Preheat oven to 325°F. Line a 15 x 10-inch jelly-roll pan with parchment paper.

2. **To make the donut holes**, microwave the rice milk and saffron threads in a 2-cup measuring cup for 20 seconds and let steep for about 2 minutes. Add the coconut nectar, coconut oil, lemon extract and stevia and stir to combine.

3. Whisk together the flour, baking powder, cardamom, guar gum and salt in a large bowl. Make a well in the middle. Add the rice milk mixture and stir to combine.

4. Take about ½ tablespoon of the dough and shape it into a ball. Place the ball on the prepared pan. Repeat until you have used up all the dough, placing the balls about 2 inches apart on the prepared pan.

5. Bake the donut holes for 11 to 12 minutes, or until they are a light golden brown and bounce back slightly to the touch. Rotate the pan from front to back after about 9 minutes of baking.

6. Transfer the pan from the oven to a wire rack and let sit for 10 minutes before removing the donut holes to cool completely.

7. **To make the saffron glaze**, microwave the rice milk, coconut nectar and saffron threads in a 2-cup measuring cup for 20 seconds. Add the powdered erythritol and salt and stir to combine.

8. Frost the donut holes with the glaze and place on the wire rack to set.

Keep in an airtight container for up to 3 days, or wrap individually and freeze for up to 3 months.

Nutrition Information Per Serving (1 donut hole): 50 calories, 2 g total fat, 0.0 mg cholesterol, 10 g carbohydrates, 40 mg sodium, 1 g fiber, 1 g protein, 3 g sugars

CHAPTER 9

OUR DAILY BREAD

It's time to take a stroll on the savory side. We think of bread as sustenance, as something to give our children as the bookends to a bountiful middle. When there are limitations to our diet for whatever the reasons, meeting nutritional needs and nibbling requirements can be easily compromised. In this chapter you will find a recipe for every day of the week that offers the health benefits and the tastes you crave. You can also count on these loaves to restore the slice to your life.

GUACAMOLE ROLLS

Makes 12 rolls

If Jefferson Starship built their city on rock and roll, just think about how much more they could have accomplished if they'd had the good sense to put it together with guac and roll. With a metropolis full of essential nutrients, phytochemicals and vitamins such as A, B, C, E and K, as well as copper, iron, phosphorous, potassium, folate, lutein and magnesium, avocado provides the building blocks for one helluva healthy superstructure. So please don't let the life-enhancing monosaturated fat count scare you away from this misunderstood fruit. Avocado is a great foundation for any salad, dip, chip and, in this case, bread roll.

MUST HAVE

*Coarse-grind cornmeal,
for dusting the muffin tin*

1¼ cups warm water (about 110°F)

2¼ teaspoons active dry yeast

1 tablespoon coconut nectar

1½ cups all-purpose gluten-free flour (see page 13)

1½ cups light buckwheat flour

4 teaspoons dried minced onion

2 teaspoons fine sea salt

½ teaspoon garlic powder

½ teaspoon baking soda

½ teaspoon ground cumin

½ teaspoon xanthan gum

2 tablespoons smoothly mashed avocado

*2 tablespoons ground chia seeds
(use a coffee grinder)*

MUST DO

1. Preheat oven to 200°F and then turn it off. Dust the wells of a standard 12-cup muffin tin with the cornmeal.

2. Combine the warm water and yeast in a 2-cup measuring cup. Add the coconut nectar and stir to combine. Let the yeast mixture sit for about 8 minutes, or until foamy.

3. Whisk together the two flours, minced onion, salt, garlic powder, baking soda, cumin and xanthan gum in a large bowl. Make a well in the middle.

4. Add the yeast mixture, mashed avocado and chia seeds and stir to combine.

5. Take about 3 tablespoons of the dough, shape it into a ball, and place it into a well of the prepared muffin tin. Repeat until you have used up all the dough.

6. Cover the muffin tin with a clean dish towel, place it in the oven for 1 hour and allow the dough balls to rise.

7. Remove the dish towel and let the dough balls continue to rise in the oven while it preheats to 425°F.

8. Bake the rolls for 25 to 27 minutes, or until they are golden brown and sound hollow when tapped on the bottom.

9. Transfer the muffin tin from the oven to a wire rack and let sit for 10 minutes before removing the rolls for a complete cooldown.

Keep the rolls in an airtight container for up to 3 days, or wrap and freeze for up to 3 months.

Nutrition Information Per Serving (1 roll):
120 calories, 1 g total fat, 0.0 mg cholesterol,
25 g carbohydrates, 400 mg sodium, 3 g fiber,
3 g protein, 1 g sugars

Sweet Truth:
People who are allergic to mustard and sesame seeds may also be allergic to chia seeds.

MULTIGRAIN LOAFER

Makes 12 round loaves

These yeasty little loaves do not loaf around when it comes to providing dynamic amino acid, mineral and vitamin essentials. The whole grains—amaranth, cornmeal and buckwheat, all of whose benefits are complex and complete—add extraordinary flavor and depth of crust. These go great with salads and soup or as a crusty snack all on their own.

MUST HAVE

*Coarse-grind cornmeal,
for dusting the muffin tin*

1¼ cups warm water (about 110°F)

2¼ teaspoons active dry yeast

1 tablespoon coconut nectar

1⅔ cups all-purpose gluten-free flour (see page 13)

⅔ cup amaranth flour

⅓ cup light buckwheat flour

⅓ cup coarse-grind cornmeal

1½ teaspoons fine sea salt

½ teaspoon baking soda

½ teaspoon xanthan gum

3 tablespoons grapeseed oil

½ teaspoon apple cider vinegar

MUST DO

1. Preheat oven to 200°F and then turn it off. Dust the wells of a standard 12-cup muffin tin with the cornmeal.

2. Combine the warm water and yeast in a 2-cup measuring cup. Add the coconut nectar and stir to combine. Let the yeast mixture sit for about 8 minutes, or until foamy.

3. Whisk together the three flours, cornmeal, salt, baking soda and xanthan gum in a large bowl. Make a well in the middle.

4. Add the yeast mixture, grapeseed oil and apple cider vinegar and stir to combine.

5. Take about 3 tablespoons of the dough, shape it into a ball, and place it into a well of the prepared muffin tin. Repeat until you have used up all the dough.

6. Cover the muffin tin with a clean dish towel, place it in the oven for 1 hour and allow the dough balls to rise.

7. Remove the dish towel and let the dough balls continue to rise in the oven while it preheats to 425°F.

8. Bake the loaves for 25 to 27 minutes, or until they are golden brown and sound hollow when tapped on the bottom.

9. Transfer the muffin tin from the oven to a wire rack and let sit for 10 minutes before removing the loaves for a complete cooldown.

Keep in an airtight container for up to 3 days, or wrap and freeze for up to 3 months.

*Nutrition Information Per Serving (1 loaf):
150 calories, 4 g total fat, 0.0 mg cholesterol,
25 g carbohydrates, 300 mg sodium, 3 g fiber,
3 g protein, 1 g sugars*

POTATO PIZZA WHEELS

Makes about 16 wheels

This recipe should be called the "Pizza Wheel Gold Rush," because neighbors will trek across acres of lawns, the challenging terrain of rosebush-lined paths and pebbled walkways to wind up at your doorstep when you make these. The combination of tomato sauce and potato spooning in this bread will leave you and your family swooning for Italy and Idaho all in the same bite.

MUST HAVE

15 x 13-inch sheet of parchment paper

Coarse-grind cornmeal, for dusting the baking sheet and cutting out the pizza wheels

1 medium russet potato (about 8 ounces)

1 cup warm water (about 110°F)

2¼ teaspoons active dry yeast

1 tablespoon coconut nectar

1½ cups all-purpose gluten-free flour (see page 13)

½ cup amaranth flour

½ cup light buckwheat flour

½ cup coarse-grind cornmeal

3 tablespoons dried minced onion

3 tablespoons dried oregano

1 tablespoon dried rosemary

1 tablespoon garlic powder

2 teaspoons fine sea salt

¾ teaspoon xanthan gum

½ teaspoon baking soda

½ cup tomato sauce

½ teaspoon apple cider vinegar

¾ cup shredded vegan, soy-free mozzarella cheese (I use Daiya mozzarella cheese. See resources for more information.)

MUST DO

1. Preheat oven to 200°F and then turn it off. Place the parchment paper on a 15 x 13-inch baking sheet and then dust evenly with cornmeal.

2. Peel the potato and cut it into ½-inch chunks. Steam the potato chunks in a medium-size saucepan for about 15 minutes, or until tender. Transfer the potato chunks to a potato ricer and push them through into a small bowl. This will give you lumpless mashed potatoes.

3. Combine the warm water and yeast in a 2-cup measuring cup. Add the coconut nectar and stir to combine. Let the yeast mixture sit for about 8 minutes, or until foamy.

4. Whisk together the three flours, cornmeal, minced onion, oregano, rosemary, garlic powder, salt, xanthan gum and baking soda in a large bowl. Make a well in the middle.

5. Add the yeast mixture, tomato sauce and apple cider vinegar and stir to combine. Fold in ¾ cup of the mashed potatoes. Next add the shredded mozzarella and mix well. The dough will be very wet and sticky at this point.

6. Take about 3 tablespoons of the dough, shape it into a ball, and place it on

the prepared baking sheet. Repeat until you have used up all the dough.

7. Flatten the balls gently with your wet hand to make disks about ½ inch thick and then use a biscuit cutter to cut out your potato pizza wheels. Use the cornmeal for easier handling.

8. When placing the wheels on the baking sheet, make sure they lie on some cornmeal so the bottoms don't stick.

9. Cover the baking sheet with a clean dish towel, place in the oven for 1 hour and allow the wheels to rise.

10. Remove the dish towel and let the wheels continue to rise in the oven while it preheats to 425°F.

11. Bake the wheels for 35 to 37 minutes, or until they are golden brown and sound hollow when tapped on the bottom.

12. Transfer the baking sheet from the oven to a wire rack and let sit for 10 minutes before removing the wheels for a complete cooldown.

Keep in an airtight container for up to 3 days, or wrap and freeze for up to 3 months.

Nutrition Information Per Serving (1 wheel): 120 calories, 3 g total fat, 0.0 mg cholesterol, 20 g carbohydrates, 300 mg sodium, 3 g fiber, 3 g protein, 2 g sugars

Sweet Truth:

For extra pizza pizzazz, top each wheel with extra sauce and cheese during the last 5 to 10 minutes of baking. You can use any tomato sauce that you know and love.

MINI BAGELS

Makes about 13 mini bagels

If you're a Jew from Queens, it is a Queensborough Bridge, Midtown Tunnel and overall tristate area requirement that you eat bagels for breakfast every Sunday morning. So that's what I did until I moved out West, got hitched and had my son. Now that all conventional bagels are considered contraband in my house, I was forced by law (see above) to figure out a way to make a wholesome, crispy and mouthwatering bagel to have for breakfast on Sundays. By hook, by crook and by throwing out a lot of gook, I came up with a recipe that passes the test and lets me back into my home state by way of the Verrazano. I'll pay the toll. Fuhget about it.

MUST HAVE

Dough

15 x 13-inch sheet of parchment paper

Coarse-grind cornmeal, for dusting the baking sheet and bagel wrangling

1¼ cups warm water (about 110°F)

1 tablespoon active dry yeast

1 tablespoon coconut nectar

2 cups all-purpose gluten-free flour (see page 13)

¾ cup tapioca flour

¼ cup amaranth flour

3 tablespoons light buckwheat flour

1 tablespoon mesquite powder

1½ teaspoons fine sea salt

1 teaspoon baking soda

1 teaspoon xanthan gum

3 tablespoons grapeseed oil

½ teaspoon apple cider vinegar

Dip

4 cups water

2 tablespoons baking soda

Toppings

Sautéed thinly sliced onion

Caraway seeds

Chia seeds

(anything goes, so use your imagination and taste buds)

MUST DO

1. Preheat oven to 200°F and then turn it off. Place the parchment paper on a 15 x 13-inch baking sheet and dust evenly with cornmeal.

2. To make the dough, combine the warm water and yeast in a 2-cup measuring cup. Add the coconut nectar and stir to combine. Let the yeast mixture sit for about 8 minutes, or until foamy.

3. Whisk together the four flours, mesquite powder, salt, baking soda and xanthan gum in a large bowl. Make a well in the middle.

4. Add the yeast mixture, grapeseed oil and apple cider vinegar and stir to combine.

5. Take about 2½ tablespoons of the dough, shape it into a ball and place it on the prepared baking sheet. Use cornmeal for easier handling. Repeat until you have used up all the dough.

6. Cover the baking sheet with a clean dish towel, place it in the oven for 1 hour and allow the dough balls to rise.

7. Take the risen dough balls out of the oven, remove the dish towel and preheat the oven to 425°F.

8. To make the dip, pour the water into a medium-size pot and bring it to a boil. Add the baking soda and stir to dissolve. Remove the pot from the heat.

9. Place the dough balls, 3 or 4 at a time, in the hot water dip for about 30 seconds, turning them once after about 15 seconds. Remove the dough balls with a slotted spatula and place them on the prepared baking sheet, rolling them in the cornmeal to make them easier to handle. Make sure each dough ball sits on some cornmeal so the bottom doesn't stick.

10. Poke a hole in the middle of each dough ball with your finger.

11. Press in the toppings of your choice and bake the bagels for 13 to 15 minutes, or until they are golden brown.

12. Transfer the baking sheet from the oven to a wire rack and let sit for 10 minutes before removing the bagels for a complete cooldown.

Keep in an airtight container for up to 3 days, or wrap and freeze for up to 3 months.

Nutrition Information Per Serving (1 bagel): 140 calories, 4 g total fat, 0.0 mg cholesterol, 23 g carbohydrates, 370 mg sodium, 3 g fiber, 3 g protein, 1 g sugars

---

Sweet Truth:

Mesquite powder not only provides a nutritional boost but also gives the bagels a gorgeous golden complexion.

PUMPCORNBREAD

Makes 16 squares

You know how people get all warm and fuzzy when waxing nostalgic about their great-grandmum's Amish corn bread recipe that's been passed down through genetics? Well, I'm not one of those people. My grandma had no time to bake, let alone eat, while running through the forests of Warsaw, with my mom dangling from her arms, to escape the Nazi evildoers, so I have no meaningful tale to tell about this pumpkin-stuffed comfort carb. All I can tell you is, I added pinches of some of my favorite spices to rev this original recipe up to a place that just feels right. Feel free to customize according to your spice threshold, and be sure to pass the recipe on to your kids so they won't call you when they're forty, and ask you to bring one over because they're hungry and waxing nostalgic about your pumpcornbread from yesteryear.

MUST HAVE

Grapeseed oil, for greasing the pan
¾ cup unsweetened plain rice milk
¼ teaspoon apple cider vinegar
1¼ cups coarse-grind cornmeal
½ cup all-purpose gluten-free flour (see page 13)
1 teaspoon sodium-free baking powder
1 teaspoon fine sea salt
½ teaspoon ground cumin
½ teaspoon ground nutmeg
¼ teaspoon guar gum
¼ teaspoon black pepper
¼ teaspoon cayenne powder
3 tablespoons grapeseed oil
3 tablespoons coconut nectar
¾ cup canned pumpkin puree

Topping
¼ cup fresh corn kernels
¼ teaspoon ground nutmeg

MUST DO

1. Preheat oven to 375°F. Grease an 8 x 8-inch square baking pan with the grapeseed oil.

2. Mix together the rice milk and apple cider vinegar in a 2-cup measuring cup.

3. Whisk together the cornmeal, flour, baking powder, salt, cumin, nutmeg, guar gum, black pepper and cayenne in a large bowl. Make a well in the middle.

4. Add the grapeseed oil, coconut nectar and pumpkin puree and stir to combine. Next add the rice milk mixture and stir until the liquid is absorbed and the batter is smooth.

5. Pour the batter into the prepared pan and smooth the top with a wet baking spatula or the back of a wet spoon. Sprinkle the corn kernels and nutmeg on top.

6. Bake the pumpcornbread for 23 to 25 minutes, or until it is a light golden brown around the edges and it starts to pull away from the sides of the pan. Rotate the pan from front to back halfway through baking.

7. Transfer the pan from the oven to a wire rack and let sit for about 20 minutes before cutting the pumpcornbread into 16 squares.

Keep in an airtight container for up to 3 days, or wrap and freeze for up to 3 months.

Nutrition Information Per Serving (1 square):
80 calories, 3 g total fat, 0.0 mg cholesterol,
15 g carbohydrates, 150 mg sodium, 2 g fiber,
2 g protein, 2 g sugars

YAM JAM SODA BREAD (MUFFINIZED)

Makes 24 mini soda breads

You don't have to be Irish to enjoy these yammy soda breads in your jammies any time of year. And since I end up eating way too much of it if left to my own loaf, I've devised these to be muffinized so everyone can have their very own mini-jam.

MUST HAVE

24 mini paper baking cups

1 small yam (about 4 ounces)

1 cup unsweetened plain rice milk

½ teaspoon apple cider vinegar

2 cups all-purpose gluten-free flour (see page 13)

½ cup amaranth flour

2 teaspoons sodium-free baking powder

1 teaspoon baking soda

1 teaspoon fine sea salt

¾ teaspoon guar gum

¼ teaspoon ground cardamom

6 tablespoons grapeseed oil

¼ cup coconut nectar

1 tablespoon plum lemon jam (see page 61)

½ cup dried currants

3 teaspoons caraway seeds

MUST DO

1. Preheat oven to 350°F. Line a 24-cup mini muffin tin with mini paper baking cups.

2. Peel the yam and slice it into ½-inch chunks. Steam the yam chunks in a medium-size saucepan for about 15 minutes, or until tender. Transfer the yam chunks to a potato ricer and push them through into a small bowl. This will give you lumpless mashed yam.

3. Mix together the rice milk and apple cider vinegar in a 2-cup measuring cup.

4. Whisk together the two flours, baking powder, baking soda, salt, guar gum and cardamom in a large bowl. Make a well in the middle.

5. Add the grapeseed oil, coconut nectar, plum lemon jam and rice milk mixture to the flour mixture, and stir until the liquid is absorbed and the batter is smooth. Fold in ⅓ cup of the mashed yam. Add ¼ cup of the currants and all the caraway seeds and mix well.

6. Spoon the batter into the prepared muffin tin, dividing it evenly. Each cup should be filled to the top. Sprinkle the remaining ¼ cup of currants on top of each cup.

7. Bake the mini soda breads for 11 to 12 minutes, or until they are a light golden brown and bounce back slightly to the touch.

8. Transfer the muffin tin from the oven to a wire rack and let sit for about 10 minutes before removing the mini soda breads for a complete cooldown.

Keep in an airtight container for up to 3 days, or wrap and freeze for up to 3 months.

Nutrition Information Per Serving (1 soda bread): 90 calories, 4 g total fat, 0.0 mg cholesterol, 15 g carbohydrates, 150 mg sodium, 2 g fiber, 2 g protein, 4 g sugars

---

KRISPY KALE 'N' CHEESE SOFT PRETZEL RODS

Makes about 16 rods

Since I'm originally from New York City, soft and salty pretzels hold a special place in my intestine. The man on the corner with the cart and the smell of roasting white dough in the middle of winter bring back a high-glycemic rush to my blood. Of course, I couldn't help but come up with a healthier but just as satisfying version. Kale is king in terms of vitamins, minerals and antioxidants. It is high in vitamins A, B_6 and C, folic acid, potassium, lutein and bioflavonoids. And when baked, kale gets irresistibly crisp. That and the crunch of caraway give a hearty nutritional bump to this supercharged hot rod.

MUST HAVE

Dough

15 x 13-inch sheet of parchment paper

Coarse-grind cornmeal, for dusting the baking sheet and rod wrangling

1¼ cups warm water (about 110°F)

4 teaspoons active dry yeast

1 teaspoon coconut nectar

2½ cups all-purpose gluten-free flour (see page 13)

1 cup tapioca flour

½ cup light buckwheat flour

¼ cup caraway seeds

2 teaspoons fine sea salt

1 teaspoon baking soda

1 teaspoon xanthan gum

¼ cup grapeseed oil

2 tablespoons coconut nectar

Dip

4 cups water

¼ cup baking soda

Topping

2 cups finely minced kale

2 cups shredded vegan, soy-free mozzarella cheese (I use Daiya mozzarella cheese. See resources for more information.)

Sheet of parchment paper (optional)

MUST DO

1. Preheat oven to 200°F and then turn it off. Place the parchment paper on a 15 x 13-inch baking sheet and dust evenly with the cornmeal.

2. To make the dough, combine the warm water and yeast in a 2-cup measuring cup. Add the coconut nectar and stir to combine. Let the yeast mixture sit for about 8 minutes, or until foamy.

3. Whisk together the three flours, caraway seeds, salt, baking soda and xanthan gum in a large bowl. Make a well in the middle.

4. Add the yeast mixture, grapeseed oil and coconut nectar and stir to combine.

5. Take about 3 tablespoons of the dough, shape it into a ball and then roll it into a rod about 3 inches long. Place the rod on the prepared baking sheet. Use the cornmeal for easier handling. Repeat until you have used up all the dough.

6. Cover the prepared baking sheet with a clean dish towel, place in the oven for 1 hour and allow the rods to rise.

7. Take the risen rods out of the oven, remove the dish towel and preheat the oven to 425°F.

8. To make the dip, pour the water into a medium-size pot and bring it to a boil. Add the baking soda and stir to dissolve. Remove the pot from the heat.

9. Place the rods, 3 or 4 at a time, in the hot water dip for about 30 seconds, turning them over once after about 15 seconds. Remove each rod with a slotted spatula and place on the prepared baking sheet.

10. To make the topping, mix together the kale and cheese, and spread the mixture out on a big sheet of parchment paper or on a cutting board. Roll one of the rods in the kale and cheese mixture until coated and until the rod is about 6 inches long. Place it back on the prepared baking sheet, making sure it rests on some cornmeal so the bottom doesn't stick. Repeat until all the rods are coated.

11. Bake the rods for 14 to 16 minutes, or until they are a light golden brown and the cheese and kale are crisp.

12. Transfer the baking sheet from the oven to a wire rack and let sit for 10 minutes before removing the rods for a complete cooldown.

Keep in an airtight container for up to 3 days, or wrap and freeze for up to 3 months.

Nutrition Information Per Serving (1 rod): 140 calories, 6 g total fat, 0.0 mg cholesterol, 20 g carbohydrates, 360 mg sodium, 3 g fiber, 3 g protein, 1 g sugars

RESOURCES

In my quest to find the cleanest, most fairly traded, most organic, least cross-contaminated ingredients, I have stumbled upon the sweetest and most caring companies that offer most everything you need to make all the recipes in this book. I am thrilled to acquaint you with:

Edison Grainery

www.edisongrainery.com

This is a family-run operation that offers grains, seeds, superfoods and flours from a nut-free, gluten-free, kosher and certified organic facility. Not only that, but their prices are very reasonable. These people are like *mishpucha* (Yiddish for "family") but nicer. You can even call them up and mix and match your orders so that they are custom made to suit your needs.

Eden Foods

www.edenfoods.com

Eden Foods sells the finest-grade organic Matcha green tea powder. They make sure the growers of these antioxidant-rich tea leaves follow strict organic farming practices for optimum flavor and nutrient retention. This company also sells dried cranberries sweetened with apple juice.

The Teff Company

www.teffco.com

Most teff comes from Ethiopia, where the conditions to grow this grain are ideal. The owner of this company realized that the climate and soil were perfect right where he was in Idaho, and he started to successfully grow teff locally. You can order his very high-quality ivory teff flour on the company website. The price can't be beat, and shipping is included.

Daiya

www.daiyafoods.com

Daiya makes the best mozzarella and cheddar cheeses that are free from dairy, casein, soy, whey and lactose, and it is all made in a facility free from milk, eggs, soy, peanuts and tree nuts. Luckily, a lot of grocery stores are starting to carry these cheeses in shredded and wedge forms.

Dakota Prairie Organic Flour Co.

www.dakota-prairie.com

Dakota Prairie mills their wide range of gluten-free flours in a dedicated facility. They carry both organic and conventional flours at very competitive prices.

Coconut Secret

www.coconutsecret.com

You will be thoroughly enlightened when you go to this website and read how the owners of Coconut Secret discovered this low-glycemic, enzyme-filled, all-natural sweetener and graced us all who use it in our daily lives. This company is my one and only source for coconut nectar.

Nutraceutical

www.nutraceutical.com

I use only KAL Pure Stevia Natural Extract, made by this company, because I find it to be superior in every way to all other brands of stevia powder on the market today.

Nutrex Hawaii

www.nutrex-hawaii.com

Hawaii is known to have the most highly nutritious, potent and pure spirulina. This company sells Hawaiian Spirulina Pacifica, which is 100 percent vegetarian and kosher, and is a non-GMO spirulina free of pesticides and herbicides.

ZSweet

www.zsweet.com

Would you ever believe that powdered "sugar" could have no sugar grams? Well, ZSweet figured out how to do it with the all-natural, zero-calorie sweeteners erythritol and stevia. All the ingredients in their powdered erythritol are gluten free, certified non-GMO, vegan, kosher and zero glycemic. You can buy it at Whole Foods, the Vitamin Shoppe or online at Amazon.

Authentic Foods

www.authenticfoods.com

This company adheres to the strictest standards for keeping their gluten-free flours just that, free from gluten. Their emphasis is on keeping ingredients nutritious and safe for celiacs. They are renowned for their superfine flours, which result in fluffy, light-textured baked goods.

Navitas Naturals

www.navitasnaturals.com

You can find your goji berry powder, goji berries, mesquite powder, chia seeds and hemp seeds here. This company is known for selling premium organic superfoods, and, boy, do they deliver on that promise!

Sambazon

www.sambazon.com

Here you can order your organic freeze-dried açaí powder. The company makes sure to use a non-thermal process of drying the berries to make a powder with maximum health benefits.

Clabber Girl

www.clabbergirl.com

Luckily, this company makes a gluten-free and sodium-free baking powder called Innova, which is produced in a nut-free facility. Now they add calcium to it to make it even healthier!

Turtle Mountain

www.sodeliciousdairyfree.com

The So Delicious yogurts are heavenly and are really what the name says they are—so delicious! I use their coconut milk plain yogurt and unsweetened coconut milk exclusively for my recipes that call for these ingredients. This company pays very close attention to the segregation of ingredients and tests its products for any traces of allergens, and they insist their co-packers do the same.

ACKNOWLEDGMENTS

Thank you to Rachel and Leo for being the giants upon whose shoulders I stood from the beginning, which allowed me to fly, fail, fluctuate, be verklempt, flop around and ultimately begin to fulfill my mission in life. I love you both more than my vocabulary allows me to express.

To my brother Barry for always being there for me, wherever "there" was, at any given moment, and for your wisdom, wit and willingness to pinch-hit in a pinch, drive when I had no car and taste test the untested experiments in the early days.

To my editor, Sarah Pelz, for her initial resounding "yes" and passionate follow-through, and for letting my idiosyncratic voice be heard.

To my extraordinary agent, Lisa Ekus, for getting in the ring, putting up her dukes and fighting on my behalf every negotiating point of the way. You're my own personal miracle worker.

To Jaimee Constantine, a big thank-you for taking care of business so seamlessly.

To Dianne Jacob, who bossed me around and kicked my keister all in the name of a worthy book proposal. Thank you for upping my writing game and for the introduction to Lisa.

To Carl Kravats, my brilliant food photographer and fellow grazer, who captured my goodies most exquisitely, beyond what I dreamed possible.

To Cindy Epstein, my food stylist, who made my baked goods look like movie stars and ready for their close-up in a most magical way.

To Mary Aalto for being my devoted recipe tester and friend.

To Maria de la Torre for cheerleading way back when and for being so graciously and selflessly helpful every step of the way. I value your friendship always.

To Pam Levin, my go-to Tilt-a-Whirl girl, for making lunch and life more fun, and for your generosity, talent and one-in-a-million sense of humor.

To Sue Saporta for being so supporta, uh, supportive, and for all the recipe testing and playdates. Thank you for your feedback, kindness and friendship.

To Elissa, my dearest friend, though farthest in distance, you're nearest at heart. Thank you for thinking I was a bitch when we were ten, but still being my friend for all these years.

To Michelle Arcilla, for your outstanding makeup and hair artistry, and for helping make me and the "gals" look glamorous in a very hot kitchen.

To my husband, who bears witness to my life every day and makes it meaningful in doing so. Thank you for your patience, your unwavering belief in all my *mishegas*, and your unconditional love.

INDEX

ABOUT THE AUTHOR

Debbie Adler is a graduate of Binghamton University and was a CPA for a large accounting firm in New York City until she realized that all she wanted to do was count to a dozen. She is now the chef and owner of Sweet Debbie's Organic Cupcakes, which caters to celebrities, Hollywood studios, large food companies and customers nationwide. Debbie lives in Los Angeles with her husband, son and raccoons that eat her garbage every night, even though she lives next door to five-star restaurant owners. Visit her website at *www.sweetdebbiesorganiccupcakes.com.*

RECIPE NOTES